BARRON'S ART HANDBOOKS

ROMANTICISM

BARRON'S ART HANDBOOKS

ROMANTICISM

BARRON'S

CONTENTS

CONTENTS

INTRODUCTION

No other movement in European art is as difficult to define as Romanticism, with its ambiguous beginnings, contradictory artistic expressions, and imprecise time frame. Several of the basic premises that gave unity to the period were inspiration in nature, an awareness of the past, a religious spirit, and an artistic ideal. Indeed, Romanticism contributed an important chapter to European culture.

The Nineteenth Century and Romanticism

From its very beginning, the nineteenth century was a difficult period, born with the legacy of the artistically significant eighteenth century, which characterized all plastic arts. It was during the nineteenth century that certain tendencies that were inherited from Neo-Classicism gave way to unrestrained Romanticism. Unlike Neo-Classicism, however, the origins and limits of Romanticism are not well-defined. Romanticism, like Neo-Classicism, spread across national boundaries. However, the Romantics' vision of objects and the world was much more sub-

The Romantic insistence on individuality and originality made the creation of a unified Romantic style impossible. However, the ideas that inspired the great Romantic artists, writers, and musicians survived their differences with enormous vigor.

jective and less rational than that of the Neo-Classicists. The movement—from academic artists such as Jacques-Louis David or Jean Auguste Dominique Ingres, to truly Romantic artists, such as Théodore Géricault or Eugène Delacroix—lasted until the arrival of Realism.

Artistic Expression and Influences

In addition to the subjects treated by the artists, Romantic sensibility also found expression in landscape painting, under the leadership of artists such as Joseph Mallord William Turner, John Constable, and Caspar David Friedrich. These artists had a major influence on other important artistic movements and currents of the time, such as the Barbizon School, whose

Joseph Vernet.
The Storm (1777).
Oil on canvas, 80 × 120.5 in.
Calvet Museum, Avignon.

members were considered precursors of French Impressionism.

The influence of Romanticism on later painting was so profound and pervasive that it is impossible to deal with it all at once. It might even be argued that in a sense all of Western art that followed Romanticism derives from this period. Romantic ideas about creativity, originality, individuality, authenticity, and integrity dominated the prevailing aesthetics of other artistic disciplines for many years.

Subsequent Evolution

Nazarenes

At the beginning of the nineteenth century a group of young German painters known as the Nazarenes combined their interest in the detailed representation of nature with a renewed interest in the religious paintings of the fourteenth and fifteenth centuries.

Pre-Raphaelites

Around the 1830s the Pre-Raphaelites in Great Britain also began to express a faithful portrayal of nature through a more precise control of line and color in their representations of objects, texture, and light.

Realists

Following the Romantic revolution, a mild reaction took place among a group of artists known as the Realists, whose motto was *il faut être de son temps* (art should be representative of its time). The idealized and fantastic elements that dominated Neo-Classical and Romantic art evoked reactions among a group of

Benjamin West. Saul and the Witch of Endor (1777).
Oil on canvas, 24.5 × 20 in. Wadsworth Atheneum, Hartford.

young artists in France who believed that artists should paint only what they could perceive through their own senses. The main proponents of this new Realism were Édouard Manet and Gustave Courbet, whose ideas and techniques contributed to the beginnings of Impressionism, the first important movement in modern art.

Symbolists

Later in the century, the Symbolists looked on the Romantics as their forerunners, although the confrontation between Symbolists and Realists reawakened a conflict that had been dormant in the artistic personalities of many individualists, such as Théodore Géricault, who was highly admired by the Realists, and Caspar David Friedrich, who was rediscovered by the Symbolists. However, while the Romantics had aimed at further exploring the relationship between reason and imagination, the tendency of their successors was to focus on both visual reality and interior vision.

Jean Auguste
Dominique Ingres.
The Turkish Bath (1862).
Oil on board, 42.5 in.
The Louvre, Paris.

THE MEANING OF ROMANTICISM

Although Romanticism was the culmination of a long period of development for tendencies and ideas that arose and coalesced from the second half of the eighteenth century on, the revolutionary nature of the movement is indisputable in that it signaled a change in the tastes and aesthetic theories of the time. The various artistic manifestations that announced the birth of the new sensibility altered prevailing tastes and opened up new possibilities for creative activity.

The Complex Definition of the Movement

While innumerable attempts have been made to define Romanticism, time and again it has proven impossible to limit the term to a series of cultural manifestations that took place within a specific framework of time or place.

When one talks about Romanticism, one is generally referring to a period spanning the last years of the eighteenth century and the first half of the nineteenth century. What is certain is that Romanticism, like Neo-Classicism that came before it and Realism that

followed, was rooted in and nourished by the culture of the eighteenth century Enlightenment. Thus, certain aesthetic modes of behavior matured along with Romanticism, as did several political events in different European countries during that period.

Rebellion and Breaking with the Past

Romanticism represented a break with tradition, with the existing order, and with the hierarchy of cultural and social values, all in the name of

genuine freedom. This break would have been impossible had it not been for the amazing and surprising nature of the movement's early artistic expressions and subsequent propagation of the Romantic spirit throughout Europe. It was a moment of passionate and contradictory protest against a capitalistic, bourgeois world and against a world of lost illusions.

Romantic Ideals

For the Romantic, only the expression of individual ideals was valid, a sensibility that

Antoine-Jean Gros. The Battle of Nazareth (1801).
Oil sketch, 76.75 × 53.25 in. Museum of Fine Art, Nantes.

Joseph Mallord William Turner. Fire at Sea *(c. 1834). Oil on canvas, 86.5 × 67.5. Tate Gallery, London.*

went beyond the limits of logical reasoning.

This was a period in which the expression of feeling dominated all else. If the revolution proclaimed political freedom, Romanticism, in turn, proclaimed freedom for artists to express their unrestrained emotions and to rid themselves of all academic influence, thereby giving free reign to spontaneity, individualism, and feeling, supreme values in Romantic art that bestowed authenticity to the artists' work.

General Characteristics

Romanticism was not a unified or uniform period. There is, however, among different artists and artistic expressions, enough commonality to refer, if not to a group, at least to a movement characterized by a certain cohesion and adherence to common ideals.

The movement is unanimous in its way of perceiving and understanding mankind, nature, and life. Many Romantic movements emerged. However, given their geographic spread, no two of these are alike.

Despite the differences that can be seen in each country, Romanticism shared several common characteristics: a feeling of spiritual anxiety in a world with which the artist could not easily identify; instability and isolation, from which arose the desire for a new social unity; an interest in the common people, their songs and legends; and the proclamation of the essential uniqueness of the individual.

Eugène Delacroix. Greece Expiring on the Ruins of Missolonghi *(c. 1826). Oil sketch on canvas, 10.75 × 16.5 in. Oskar Reinhart "Am Römerholz" Collection, Winterthur.*

THE ROMANTIC SPIRIT

Feeling and individualism, characteristics that defined the essential nature of Romanticism, arose when Neo-Classicism was in full flourish. Circumstances changed in the early years of the nineteenth century and other energies, arising from ideas that had led to the change from the ancient to the new regime, had begun to spread. The artistic ideal no longer focused on the rational but on the personal and the original.

Jacques-Louis David. The Love of Paris and Helen. (1788) Oil on canvas, 71.25 × 57.5 in. Louvre Museum, Paris.

Romanticism and the Enlightenment

Romanticism could be defined as a critical moment in the conscience of the Enlightenment. Elements of the Romantic spirit, such as a longing for the Middle Ages and for distant, exotic lands, or the exaltation of the infinite, of dreams, the occult and the night, already existed in the eighteenth century. Romanticism gave a different response to this type of situation than had been given by what was considered the cold Neo-Classicism of Jacques-Louis David. The Enlightenment signified awareness of philosophical knowledge and drive toward scientific progress.

Thanks to John Locke and Anthony Ashley Cooper Shaftes-bury, the philosophy of the Enlightenment re-established the *status* of the human being as the first object of knowledge and as a subject capable of dominating nature by analyzing information obtained through the senses in an effort to attain truth.

Locke assumed that all knowledge derives from perceived experience, either acquired through the senses or reflection, giving rise to individual ideas; Shaftesbury, his pupil, attempted to develop in his work an individual and social moral ideal based on the harmonious development of personality.

Nonconformist Tendency

The Romantic artist is a unique individual who is characterized not only by his rebellion against the order of the world he inherited from his predecessors, but also by his opposition toward the separation of reason and feeling, the real and the unreal. For the Romantic, the essence of being human goes beyond what is conscious and rational. In this sense, it is argued that the Romantics were the discoverers of the unconscious because of their notion of new forces acting within them. The Romantic is the prototype of the nonconformist and the rebel, and to a certain extent represents a new interpretation of the conflict stated by Diderot

Honoré Daumier. The Load (undated). Oil on canvas, 18 × 21.75 in. Národni Gallery, Prague.

(1713–1784) between *natural man* and *moral man*, a conflict that recognizes the contradiction between internal feelings and rational sense. The Romantic ego refuses to be just part of the machinery of nature. On the contrary, it proclaims its individuality and capacity for creation and transformation, which comes from within and allows it to fight for its beliefs.

The First Romantic Painters

The first changes that signaled a new direction in art took place in the studio of Jacques-Louis David (1748–1825). François Gérard (1770–1837), a student of David since 1786, also followed this direction, though he differed from David in his use of composition and color that characterized both his mythological and historical paintings. Anne-Louis Girodet de Roncy (1767–1824), a favorite pupil of David and also known as Girodet-Trioson, also followed the new direction. Her paintings were dedicated to subjects of ancient history, Napoleon's exploits, and subjects from contemporary literature. Together with Gérard, she decorated the castle of Malmaison in 1801. Pierre Paul Prud'hon (1758–1823), another artist in the new vein, saw the works of Neo-Classical artists such as Mengs, Kauffman, and Canova in Rome. When he returned to Paris in 1789, he joined the revolutionary fervor and the "Club des Arts."

Antoine-Jean Gros (1771–1835), another of David's pupils, committed suicide after years of loneliness, lack of recognition, and being overcome by the new trends in painting. Meanwhile, important contributions to aesthetic theory and Romanticism were being made in Germany by Wincklemann in art, Lessing in literature, and Goethe in poetry.

Pierre Paul Prud'hon. The Triumph of Bonaparte (1800). Oil sketch, 46.25 × 35.5 in. Fine Art Museum, Lyons.

NEO-CLASSICISM AND ROMANTICISM

In Neo-Classicism, artists wanted to render a perfect world through integrity and a high sense of morality, adapting models from Greek and Classical antiquity. The main difference between Romantic art and Neo-Classical art was that the principal criterion for Romantic artists was their own sensibility and for Neo-Classical artists it was their desire to express traditional values. While both movements began during the eighteenth century and continued until the nineteenth century, Neo-Classicism is identified with reason and Romanticism with feelings and passion.

Study of the Term Neo-Classicism

Art defined as Neo-Classical pays homage to its roots in Greco-Roman history, literature, and art. Classical themes and motifs had been fundamental to the plastic arts (three-dimensional art, such as sculpture) from the time of the Renaissance, although Neo-Classicism is distinguished by its deliberate selection of subject matter. However, the inspiration of Classical antiquity was expressed in contrasting ways as evidenced, for example, in the work by Jean-Baptiste Greuze (1725–1805), *The Father's Curse*, which was based partly on classical sculpture, or in the Homeric engravings of John Flaxman (1755–1826), which were inspired by the figures on Greek vase paintings and statues. Most artists in the Romantic period whose work was openly Greco-Roman in

form or subject matter also expressed themselves in other styles. Flaxman also produced illustrations for works by Dante Alighieri and was inspired by Italian Gothic art, while David painted scenes of ostentatious contemporary life in a style derived from Rubens' baroque paintings.

> The term Neo-Classicism describes a type of constant inspiration rooted in the Greco-Roman past, which always had been a source of inspiration to Western artists.

Study of the Term Romanticism

The term Romanticism refers to the deep fascination that non-classical literature and history held over artists from

1770. It is also defined as a state of feelings that describe a situation of emotional anxiety that seemed to become more intense with the passage of time until it reached its culmination in the decade of the 1820s.

This description covers a wide range of tendencies, from the urgent desire for exploration, at least in the imagination, of the far-off worlds of exotic or primitive societies, to passionate declarations on public morality.

The World of Fantasy

The interpretation of individualism, in its subjective sense, opened the way for the work of the more revolutionary European Romantic artists. Their subject matter was the state of the hallucinating mind, an attraction to the medieval world, fantasy, abnormality, madness, and the irrational. This vision can be found in the work of Johann Heinrich Füssli (1741–1825), a Briton of Swiss origin, and in the painting of William Blake (1757–1827), who was also British, and who, in his watercolors, shows a poetical world brimming with a literature of magical visions and occultism, as well as with characters extracted from his

Jean-Baptiste Greuze.
The Father's Curse (c. 1765).
Oil on canvas, 64.75 × 51.25 in.
The Louvre, Paris.

Jacques-Louis David.
The Sabine Women *(1799). Oil on canvas, 205.5 × 151.5 in. The Louvre, Paris.*

own mythological world and fantasy. His influence is evident in other painters such as Samuel Palmer (1805–1881).

Belonging to the same imaginative inferno are most of the works by Francisco de Goya (1746–1828), whose pictorial universe is one of madmen, bandits, the plague stricken, martyrs, massacres, kidnappers, and killers, and who, in his *Black Paintings*, depicted the most fascinating world found in all of Romanticism.

The World of Reality

The Romantic spirit of individualism is also found in the significance that several Romantic artists gave to contemporary political events, a significance that found expression as a response to the coercion that the new liberal bourgeoisie imposed on the freedoms proclaimed by the Revolution of 1789.

In this period of great moral contradictions, most Romantic artists were not indifferent to the contemporary liberal revolutionary or patriotic movements through which they lived. The paintings of Théodore Géricault (1791–1824) are a good example of this, as are those of Eugène Delacroix (1798–1863), who also lived through this period and who demonstrated his commitment to this time through his works.

Joseph Mallord William Turner. The Slave Ship *(1839–1840). Oil on canvas, 48 × 35.5 in. Museum of Fine Arts, Boston.*

ATTITUDE TOWARD NATURE

Romantic art argued for the revival of the feeling of wonder toward nature that
Neo-Classicism had, for the most part, relegated to a secondary position
in life. Nature was represented either as an idyllic, serene state, or, on the
contrary, as an indomitable force, although artists always attempted to depict
a version of it that was quite alien to the safe and placid bourgeois world.

Pictorial Themes

Landscapes played an important role in many works of the
late eighteenth and early
nineteenth centuries, reflecting
the prevailing spirit of the
times. Themes such as dusk,
night, moonlight, and so on
were the perfect excuse to
convert landscape into a vehicle
for pictorial or emotional exploration, as represented, for
example, in the works of the
German artist Caspar David
Friedrich (1774–1840).

Given the tendency of artists
to search for sublime experiences of awe, one of the most
important new themes in landscape painting was the splendor
of the mountains. This vision of
nature was adorned with ruins
and remains from the past that
symbolized the unforgiving
passage of time and thus, as a
consequence, the very weak-
ness of the human being.

The artists who best conveyed
this Romantic attitude toward
nature were Friedrich, mentioned earlier, and the British
artist Joseph Mallord William
Turner (1775–1851). Friedrich
was the leading figure in
German Romantic landscape
painting. His work is notable for
its use of art as an intermediary
between man and nature, where
landscapes do not reflect a
specific place but rather a
mystical-psychological state in
which there is an implicit
philosophical meditation on
the destiny of man.

Masters of British Landscape

With Turner, nature became
a theme for splendid visions
that he transformed into something exceptional. Besides this
type of landscape, full of passion and drama, there also
emerged another way of addres-
sing nature, based on a particular, complicit understanding
between artist and natural
reality. This artistic point of
view was known as the
Poetics of Painting, an imaginative, naturalist current that
gave rise to the birth of Romantic landscape painting in
Great Britain.

All the great British landscape
painters who are considered
part of the Romantic movement
belonged to the last generation

Joseph Mallord William Turner.
Saint-Germain-en-Laye.
Watercolor, 180 × 117.75 in. The Louvre, Paris.

French Artists

The influence of Constable among artists of this period was important, but much more significant for the future of the Romantic-Naturalist landscape genre was the so-called Barbizon School of French landscape painters whose works reflected a synthesis between the Romantic spirit and the demands of reality.

With time, their deep feeling for the reality of nature was articulated through a realistic detail that often confused the viewer. However, this was not the case with Paul Huet (1803–1869), whose work displays a very strong Romantic character, or with Virgile Narcisse Diaz de la Peña (1807–1867). It is the case with the group who showed solidarity and great devotion to the exceptional Théodor Rousseau (1812–1884). Along with Rousseau one must mention other artists like Jules Dupré (1811–1884), Constant Troyon (1810–1865) and, from 1849, Jean François Millet (1814–1875).

Thomas Girtin. The Shimmering Crag (Bamburgh Castle, Northumberland) *(c. 1797). Watercolor, 17.75 × 21.5 in. Tate Gallery, London.*

of the eighteenth century: John Crome (1768–1821), Thomas Girtin (1775–1802), John Constable (1776–1837) and Turner. Transcending the rigorous rules set forth by the patriarch of landscape painting, Richard Wilson (1713–1782), the landscape paintings of John Robert Cozens (1725–1797) and John Crome moved toward the exaltation of light and harmonious space.

Richard Wilson. Croome Court, Worcestershire *(1758). Oil on canvas, 247.25 × 199.5 in. Wadsworth Atheneum, Hartford.*

SENSE OF RELIGION AND MYSTICISM

The religious and mystical impulse that Romanticism experienced at the end of the eighteenth century and the beginning of the nineteenth century, thanks to the support of writers such as Wackenroder, Novalis, Tieck, the Schlegels, and Chateaubriand, led to the recovery of the Christian faith and to religious paintings. The religion of the Romantics was based on an essential intuition of the divine and coincided, in many ways, with the spirituality of the Christian Middle Ages.

The Figure of Chateaubriand

The publication in France of *Atala* (1801) and *The Genius of Christianity* (1802), by the writer, soldier, traveler, ambassador, and minister François-René de Chateaubriand (1768–1848), the creator of the French Romantic School, was like a starter pistol that juxtaposed the drama of Christian religion to the rationalist atheism of Neo-Classicism, replacing pagan myth with stories of the evangelists and the lives of the saints, and the Greek temple with the Gothic cathedral, symbol of the divine presence, and the pre-eminence of the power of the Church.

Nevertheless, it is practically impossible to view the religious character of certain Romantic artistic works from a single perspective.

An example of this is the work *The Entombment of Atala* (1808), by Anne-Louis Girodet de Roncy (Girodet-Trioson) who expressed in this painting the ideas and feelings of Chateaubriand.

Chateaubriand, exalting Christianity and using the Middle Ages as an example, tried to justify its great contribution to human history, especially in the fields of artistic and literary expression.

Jean Auguste Dominique Ingres. Pope Pius VII in the Sistine Chapel *(1814).*
Oil on canvas, 365 × 293.25 in. National Gallery of Art, Washington, D.C.

Attitude Toward Nature
Sense of Religion and Mysticism
Fervor for the Middle Ages and for the East

17

Official Commissions

During the period of the Restoration, the new Romantic movement triumphed fully, a situation that brought with it the official commissioning of many works by the monarchy. Among works that exalted the simplicity and virtue of the Bourbons, a large number of works were commissioned to decorate churches that had been destroyed during the time of the Revolution. Some of the churches commissioned famous painters, but many others commissioned mediocre painters rooted in academic tradition. This type of painting was not very pleasant work to do, given that it did not have the importance of traditional historical painting.

Literature and German Art

The publication of *Outpourings of an Art-Loving Monk* (1797), by Wilhelm Heinrich Wackenroder, whose ideas were shared by the poets Ludwig Tieck and Friedrich Leopold von Hardenberg (known as Novalis), by the Schlegel brothers, by Friedrich Wilhelm Joseph von Schelling, and by Georg Friedrich Hegel, announced the reawakening of Christianity in Germany and, in the purist Nazarene movement led by Friedrich Overbeck (1789–1869), of the purest expression of Christian spiritualist art in the Romantic period.

Claudio Lorenzale.
Allegory of Winter
(c. 1857). Oil on canvas,
33.5 × 41.75 in.
Museum of Modern Art,
Barcelona.

The Influence of the Nazarenes

The religious and mystic reaction represented by this group of painters, who included Peter Cornelius (1783–1867), Julius Schnorr von Caroldsfeld (1794–1872), and Karl Philipp Fohr (1795–1818), impressed a group of painters from Barcelona, Spain, who, arriving in Rome in 1830, became passionate followers of Overbeck and his ideas. This group of artists, who include the theoretician Pau Milà i Fontanals and the painters Claudio Lorenzale (1816–1889), Pelegrí Clavé (1811–1880), and Joaquim Espalter (1809–1880), founded the purist aesthetic in Barcelona. In Rome, an Italian follower of the German idealist doctrines was the painter Tommaso Minardi (1787–1871), who was in close contact with the Barcelona painters.

The German Otto Runge (1777–1810), expressed his religious spirit through an intimate communion with nature. He was connected to the group of writers, critics, and men of letters from Dresden, such as Heinrich von Kleist and, most of all, with the poet Tieck, as well as with other painters such as the Norwegian Johan Christian Clausen Dahl (1788–1857) and Georg Friedrich Kersting (1785–1847).

Anne-Louis Girodet-Trioson.
The Entombment
of Atala (1808). Oil on
canvas, 105.25 × 82.75 in.
The Louvre, Paris.

THE ROMANTIC MOVEMENT

FERVOR FOR THE MIDDLE AGES AND FOR THE EAST

An interest in the Middle Ages was another of the sources of inspiration for the Romantic artist. It was a case of escapism through time, provoked by a state of dissatisfaction that gripped a generation that had witnessed the turn of the century and had been suffocated by the falseness of revolutionary ideals and by the optimism that for years had captivated the most sensitive among them in the face of the social and moral problems of contemporary society.

The Search for Lost Ideals

The interest in the Middle Ages represented a stand against the ideological system and bourgeois culture that had aided the establishment of a reactionary regime entirely lacking in humanitarian ideals.

An escape route to contemporary reality was sought and this was found in an age that seemed to incarnate the lost ideals: the Middle Ages, the time of the knights who fought in the Holy Land or of the Gothic cathedrals that summarized the spirit of militant Christianity praised by Victor Hugo in *Nôtre Dame de Paris* (1831).

The establishment of the Middle Ages in the nineteenth century became a passionate Romantic enthusiasm.

Works on medieval themes in troubadour-style painting created a highly anecdotal genre, halfway between history and genre painting, whose best exponents were in France.

The East

The attraction of marketplaces and mosques, the streets of ancient Muslim cities and the extensive deserts of sand bathed in sunshine fascinated the Europeans of the nineteenth century.

Orientalism thus became, together with landscape and historical painting, one of the most genuine expressions of Romanticism. The reasons for this art trend can be found, on the one hand, in the development of commerce and the political vicissitudes of the century that saw the onset of European colonization, and on the other hand, in the appearance and influence of literature on an Oriental theme that stimulated a thirst for exoticism and poured out effusive praise for the worlds of the sultans and pashas.

Spread of Orientalism in France and Great Britain

Both in France and in Great Britain, the interest in Orientalism was spurred by the publications of François-René de Chateaubriand, George Gordon (Lord Byron), Thomas Moore, and A.W. Kinglake. However, Orientalism had the most influence in France.

*Eugène Fromentin.
A Falcon Hunt
in Algeria (1863).
Oil on canvas,
46.5 × 63.75 in.
Musée d'Orsay, France.*

Sense of Religion and Mysticism **19**
Fervor for the Middle Ages and for the East
Respect for the Past and Attitude of the Artist

Among the painters who portrayed their vision of the East are Eugène Delacroix, Eugène Fromentin (1820–1876), Alexandre Gabriel Decamps (1803–1860), the British artists John Frederick Lewis (1805–1876), and the pre-Raphaelite William Homan Hunt (1827–1910). A late representative of Orientalist painting was Marià Fortuny (1838–1874), born in Reus (Spain).

Among all those who painted from literature or the imagination, one must mention Delacroix, with his *Death of Sardanapal* (1814), or Jean Auguste Dominique Ingres, with his *Grande Odalisque* (1814). Another important figure was Richard Parkes Bonington (1802–1826), an excellent British landscape painter who produced magnificent Oriental prints, or the French artist Antoine-Jean Gros, who painted his *Napoleon Visiting the Plague Stricken at Jaffa* (1804) in an Oriental style, despite never having been to the East.

Jean Auguste Dominique Ingres. The Dream of Ossian (1813).
Oil on canvas, 104.25 × 137 in. The Louvre, Paris.

Antoine-Jean Gros. Napoleon Visiting the Plague Stricken at Jaffa (1804).
Oil on canvas, 720 × 523 in. The Louvre, Paris.

RESPECT FOR THE PAST AND ATTITUDE OF THE ARTIST

The ideas held at the beginning of the nineteenth century on the Middle Ages were developed more deeply and expressed over time in numerous Romantic works. Other periods in Western history also found followers among the Romantic artists, who placed personal liberty of expression above prescribed rules or codes.

The French Revolution and Social Classes

The French Revolution heightened the sense of history in a way that no other event had ever done in the past. By opening up a chasm between the present and the immediate past, a chasm that seemed to grow larger with every year between 1789 and 1815, it had the effect of accelerating an awareness of the passing of time.

The transition from the eighteenth to the nineteenth century could not just be felt but could even be seen by

every social class throughout Europe, although nowhere as clearly as in France, where it was even visible in clothing and hairstyles. The custom of commenting on current events through paintings whose subjects were set in distant times was frequently used during the Revolution and the Empire.

Meanwhile, a tendency emerged to search for parallels in the past instead of for precedents and moral examples. This, perhaps, is the reason for the popularity of Henry IV, who two centuries earlier had brought peace to France by

uniting Catholics and Protestants. It is possible that this tendency to find similarities in the past might seem contradictory with the awareness that people from other periods felt, thought, and acted in a different way, and therefore, had to be judged in the context of the values of their times, although in fact the two positions are complementary.

Survival of Tastes

The history of tastes in interior decoration and the decorative arts during this period is very instructive. The Imperial style survived throughout the whole of continental Europe for more than a decade after 1815. Nevertheless, if there was one style that predominated between 1820 and 1840, it was possibly an ornate Neo-Rococo, a style against which the more serious designers rebelled by returning to sixteenth century tastes. Artists also imitated objects from Greek and Roman antiquity.

Whether in a Classical, Medieval, Renaissance, or eighteenth-century style, these objects generally show evidence of a careful study of prototypes that were illustrated in a growing number of books. Buildings and decorative elements that are most often related to Romanticism are those in a

Théodore Géricault.
An Officer of the Imperial Horse Guards Charging *(1812).*
Oil on canvas, 76.5 × 115 in.
The Louvre, Paris.

Fervor for the Middle Ages and for the East
Respect for the Past and Attitude of the Artist
The Spread of Romanticism

21

John Constable. The Haywain *(1824). Oil on canvas, 72.75 × 51.25 in. National Gallery, London.*

Neo-Gothic style and, in the case of historical paintings, those with Medieval or sixteenth-century themes.

The paintings inspired by the archaeological remains found at Pompeii and Herculaneum displayed not only the architecture of antiquity and the interest in this period, but also topics such as the ignorance, superstition, vice, and cruelty of the ancient world.

Artistic Freedom

What most concerned Romantic artists was their personal freedom, as well as freedom from rules prescribed by academies and the capriciousness of patrons.

The new awareness that artists had of themselves and their originality was most explicitly shown in self-portraits. Writers and musicians were portrayed in the same way: distanced from the world, as if they were above conventional, formal norms.

Illustrations of scenes in the lives of artists became very popular during the first half of the nineteenth century in Germany, Italy, and especially in France, as were episodes linked to Christopher Columbus and the life of the poet Torquato Tasso. Even so, among the historical or fictional characters with whom the Romantics identified themselves, none was as revealing as the figure of Don Quixote.

Francisco de Goya. The Witches' Sabbath *(1819–1823).*
Wall mural transposed onto canvas, 171.5 × 55 in. The Prado, Madrid.

THE SPREAD OF ROMANTICISM

Romanticism spread widely throughout Europe and many top-rank artists made this movement into a new way of life. Along with them, more mediocre painters also contributed through their work to the expansion and recognition of the more famous Romantics. Both groups, starting from more or less similar premises, helped each country to express its particular Romantic vision from its own ideological and artistic point of view.

France

In France, in the shadow of great masters like Jean Auguste Dominique Ingres, Théodore Géricault, and Eugène Delacroix, many works were created by a great number of artists. Most of these are of less importance, particularly painters of historical themes such as Paul Delaroche (1797–1856), Ary Scheffer (1795–1858), or Eugène Devéria (1805–1865). Among this mediocre group stand out Théodore Chassériau (1819-1856) and Horace Vernet (1789-1863), a talented painter who extolled the history of France in dramatic, pompous tones.

Spain

Except for the works of Francisco de Goya, Romanticism came late to Spain compared with the rest of Europe. As the genre literature of the period reflects, this type of painting had two different centers of activity, Seville and Madrid, each with its own characteristics.

The former, rooted in the tradition of Murillo, showed a tendency for a warm palette and clean colors but conveyed a false vision of Andalucia. Out of this group of painters stand out the Dominguez Bécquer family, José (1805–1845), his nephew Joaquín (1817–1879),

and his son Valeriano (1833–1870), as well as José Roldán y Martínez (1806–1871) and others.

The Madrid-based painters followed the popular tradition of Goya. In this Madrid group are included José Elbo (1804–1844) and Leonardo Alenza. Other important figures in Spanish Romanticism were Federico Madrazo (1815–1894) and Carlos Luis Ribera (1815–1891).

Great Britain

All styles of painting were practiced in Great Britain. The greatest interest was for historic and folkloric painting, although the portrait and the

Horace Vernet. Ballad of Leonore (1839).
Oil on canvas, 21.5 × 24 in.
Fine Art Museum, Nantes.

Leonardo Alenza. The Revenge.
Oil on canvas, 9.75 × 13 in.
The Prado, Casón del Buen Retiro, Madrid.

Paul Delaroche. The Execution of Lady Jane Grey (1834). Oil on canvas, 117 × 96.75 in. National Gallery, London.

landscape were not ignored. In the first category, John Singleton Copley (1738–1815) and James Northcote (1746–1831) deserve a mention, while the genre painters include the artist David Wilkie (1785–1841).

Germany

In Germany, the influence of the Düsseldorf School was partly responsible for the pictorial output of local Romanticism, in many cases crossing the borders to influence the development of Scandinavian, Austrian, and Swiss painters. The most important figure, apart from the members of the Nazarenes who returned to their native land, was the landscape painter Carl Friedrich Lessing (1808–1880).

Along with Lessing, Alfred Rethel (1816–1859), painted bombastic historical themes, such as scenes from the life of Charlemagne for the Aachen City Hall. Among the Nazarenes, the figure of Adrian Ludwig Richter (1803–1884) stands out as a true Romantic in his portrayal of Italian landscapes and genre scenes.

Italy

In Italy, the best representative of Romantic painting was the Venetian Francesco Hayez (1791–1882). Trained in Rome, he established himself in Milan in 1820 where he became the most important figure among a group of painters who followed the inspiration of Romanticism.

Adrian Ludwig Richter. Crossing the River at Schreckenstein bei Aussig (1837). Oil on canvas, 61.75 × 46 in. Staatliche Kunstsammulungen, Gemäldegalerie, Neue Meister, Dresden.

THE PICTORIAL SCHOOL
OF GREAT BRITAIN

The search for new sensations accelerated toward the end of the eighteenth century, both in the public arena of official exhibitions and in the personal and individual inner world of the most inquiring artists of the time. Nevertheless, the artists found a suitable path for total artistic expression and growth, while at the same time appealing to public taste.

The Precedent of Goya and the Work of Johann Füssli

The work of Goya displays the conflict between the traditional obligation of the artist to reflect official and public ideals, and his personal need to explore a world that was private and irrational. This was a common dilemma among many artists of his generation, as well as among subsequent generations, and it was a conflict that was particularly intense in the world of British art. In works like *Watson and the Shark* (1778) by the previously mentioned John Singleton Copley, or *The Indian Widow* (1783–1785) by Joseph Wright, the viewer was offered a new type of sensation, one that was extraordinarily strong in the form of pictorial expression of the

Johann Heinrich Füssli. The Nightmare *(1781). Oil on canvas, 50 × 40 in. Institute of Arts, Detroit.*

portrayed themes.

One of the pioneers of this exploration of the irrational was Johann Heinrich Füssli, who, after his return to London in 1779, enthused the public with

John Singleton Copley. Watson and the Shark *(1778). Oil on canvas, 90.25 × 71.75 in. Museum of Fine Arts, Boston.*

George Stubbs. Horse Attacked by a Lion *(1770). Oil on canvas. Yale University Art Gallery, New Haven.*

an extensive exhibition in which he gave form to his dreams.

In his work, the images distance themselves from Renaissance canons of perspective to move into the realms of the irrational, while the forms of his figures invent new beings of sensual fantasy.

George Stubbs

Not all artists needed literary texts or an abstraction of style to immerse themselves further in the world of the irrational. Some, like George Stubbs (1724–1806), the best painter of animals of the eighteenth century, could work with examples that were so real that his paintings and drawings often showed a great scientific precision and thus became interesting zoological documents. In his *Horse Attacked by a Lion,* he combined shadowy natural spaces with the reality of the white horse being attacked by the lion. Nevertheless, he also tried to recover the wilder side of nature, representing exotic beasts in a natural environment.

For Stubbs, as for many artists at the beginning of the nineteenth century dedicated to painting the realities of nature, there was no distinction between the meticulous representation of real details of nature and the subsequent expression of wonder at these phenomena of earthly life.

Philip Reinagle

In a deeper exploration of the topic of animals in their natural environment, the work of Philip Reinagle (1749–1833) clearly represents the terrifying extremes of fantasy and terror that the artists of Great Britain had attained at the turn of the century while influenced by the philosopher Edmund Burke. Similarly, Benjamin West

had begun the decade of the 1770s exploring the possibilities of the sublime through art, with themes that recurred frequently over his long artistic career.

The Figure of William Blake

The intensity and magnitude of the vision of the poet, painter, and engraver William Blake were perhaps unique, although his contemporaries in Great Britain and on the European continent shared many aspects of his concept of art. The German artist of his generation, Asmus Jacob Carstens (1754–1798) was one such contemporary.

Like Füssli and John Flaxman, Blake was sensitive to the influence of the cultural environment that was closely linked to the classicist myths of the eighteenth century and to proto-Romantic tendencies. He was also an innovative poet and visionary.

JOSEPH MALLORD WILLIAM TURNER

The consequences of integrating man with nature, together with the linking of nature to the state of mind and aesthetic sense of the human being, became a fundamental element in the attitude of the artist who wanted to express his feelings through nature rather than just imitate it, and who focused his sensations on specific places and not on nature as a whole. These concerns are exceptionally well represented in the works of the two greatest British Romantic painters: Joseph Mallord William Turner and John Constable.

The Man and His Beginnings As an Artist

Encouraged by his father, who despite his precarious economic situation helped him attend the painting school of the Royal Academy in 1790, Turner became, along with Constable, in time, a great student of the phenomena of the sky and of natural light, although the two artists had very different aims. A pupil of John Robert Cozens, Turner initially dedicated himself to watercolor in the belief that he would specialize in illustration. However, he would go on to create one of Romanticism's most personal visions of land-

Joseph Mallord William Turner. Fleet on the River Tyne *(1823). Watercolor. Clore Gallery for the Turner Collection (Great Britain).*

Joseph Mallord William Turner. The Burning of the Houses of Lords and Commons, 16th October 1834 *(1835). Oil on canvas, 47.75 × 35.5 in. Philadelphia Museum of Art.*

scape. Nicolas Poussin and Claude Lorrain had a great influence on his work. Even so, without discounting the lessons learned from these and other masters of the past, Turner progressively developed his own personal style, a style in which atmosphere and light were the objects of ever greater attention and careful detail.

Greatest Work and Subsequent Influence

When Turner painted Admiral Nelson's old ensign ship *Temeraire* on its way to the scrap yard, the result was a melancholy symbol of fate, laden with the same force of expression as the ships of Caspar David Friedrich when they sail out of sight beyond the horizon. Masterpieces such as *Interior at Petworth* or *The Burning of the Houses of Lords and Commons* appeared progressively from then on. In the 1840s, in the last decade of his life, Turner managed to represent in the most surprising manner themes that obsessed

Joseph M. W. Turner. Rain, Steam and Speed—The Great Western Railway *(1844). Oil on canvas, 48.5 × 35.75 in. National Gallery, London.*

him, such as the sublime power of nature or the poetic connotations of a boat in peril as a symbol of the destiny of man.

Turner was one of the most important colorists in the history of Western art. He influenced the French Impressionists, especially in his "unfinished" works, which led them to their own interpretations of reality, and

his innovative principles in the arrangement of color fore-shadowed the chromatic theories of the twentieth century.

He increasingly isolated himself during his final years. His paintings became more and more focused on his personal and unique vision of light and color and on the ways of reproducing them in painting.

THE ARTIST'S LIFE

1775 Born in London to a family of limited financial means.	**1802** Makes a journey to Paris and Switzerland.	**1829** Returns to Italy.
1790 Begins his studies at the painting school of the Royal Academy.	**1815** Completes *Dido building Carthage* or *The Rise of the Carthaginian Empire.*	**1834** The small sketches he had made of the spectacular fire that destroyed the Houses of Parliament in London are turned into paintings.
1794 Exhibits for the first time at the Academy School.	**1819** Travels to France, Switzerland, the Rhine Valley, and Italy, where he visits Venice, Rome, and Naples. This journey represents a fundamental stage in his artistic work.	**1840–1842** His rejection of the visible world makes his landscapes increasingly vague, turning them into representations of unreal worlds.
1796 In addition to water-color and engraving, his first forms of artistic expression, he also dedicates himself to oil paints.		
1800 Is elected member of the Royal Academy where he teaches for thirty years.	**1820** His oil paintings are accused of not being finished, although this characteristic makes him the most important painter of his time.	**1846** Lives removed from the world, under a false name, investigating the phenomena of light. **1851** Dies in his native city of London, in total solitude.

JOHN CONSTABLE

Constable was a painter whose work was committed to the constant and profound study of nature and which had a literary equivalent in the poetry of Wordsworth. His work was not based on a generic and idealized form of nature, but rather on the depiction of landscape as a beautiful place seen in a specific season at a specific hour of the day, and in well-defined light and atmospheric conditions. His constant return to the same themes reveals the depth of his artistic analysis.

Constable's Theoretical View

Constable was an intuitive painter and artist who, at the age of twenty-one, had to set aside his vocation in order to help his father in his work as a miller. In 1799 he moved to London, where the following year he was able to enter the Royal Academy as a student. His interest in landscape led him to study classical landscape artists such as Claude Lorrain, Nicolas Poussin, and Gaspard Dughet, the Dutch painters of the sixteenth century, and the British artists Thomas Girtin, Thomas Gainsborough, John Robert Cozens, and Richard Wilson. But what he admired most of all was nature, which he had studied profoundly during his childhood. In essence he was more of a Realist than a Romantic. This is why in his landscapes he ignored any element that was foreign to the realistic representation of nature, elements that even in the artists whom he most admired appear

John Constable. Study of Clouds *(c. 1821–1822). Oil on paper, 70 × 45 in. Victoria and Albert Museum, London.*

in a conventional way in the conception of the composition. He sought compositional rhythm by means of extensive studies and meditative contemplation and through making repeated sketches of the chosen theme.

Sensibility and Landscape As Subject

Inspired by places to which he often returned several years hence to paint the same scenes, among his most outstanding paintings are the views he painted of Hampstead Heath and Salisbury Cathedral.

His place of birth also offered him an unending source of subject matter, which he translated into some of his most famous works, such as *Flatford Mill* or *The Haywain*. During his travels he drew notes from life—the Victoria and Albert Museum in London

John Constable. Hampstead Heath *(1819). Oil on canvas, 263 × 150.5 in. Tate Gallery, London.*

John Constable. Salisbury Cathedral from the Meadows *(1831).*
Oil on canvas, 72.5 × 58.75 in. Private Collection.

has his notebooks from 1813 and 1814—and most of which he later used to make small sketches that in turn he transformed into larger oil paintings until he had achieved the highly detailed version of the definitive work.

Constable's Contribution

Constable's contribution to European painting was, over time, extremely positive. It consisted basically of something so simple as the freedom to observe and interpret the natural qual-

ities of light according to a scale of color that was much more exact and harmonious than anything that had been seen before that time.

For this reason, a damp luminosity seems to wrap his works in an atmosphere full of life.

THE ARTIST'S LIFE

1776 Born in East Bergholt, Suffolk (Great Britain), a region to which he remained emotionally tied his entire life.

1795 Visits the English capital regularly.

1799 Moves to London to study at the Royal Academy.

1802 Exhibits at the salon of the Royal Academy, and seven years later is elected to the title of scholar of the institution.

1819 Travels to Venice and Rome, where he is

named an associate member of the Royal Academy.

1820 His paintings begin to win increasing recognition.

1821 His work *The Haywain*, exhibited under the title *Landscape at Noon,* is a great success at the Paris Salon.

1824 His work is a great success at the Paris Salon, and influences Delacroix and the landscape painters of the Barbizon School.

1825 Wins the Gold Medal of the Paris Salon.

1828 The death of his wife condemns him to a life of depression and loneliness.

1829 Following numerous rejections, he is finally elected a member of the Royal Academy.

1835–1836 Family and health problems influence the darkening tone of his paintings.

1837 Dies in London.

THE SUCCESSORS TO JACQUES-LOUIS DAVID

At the turn of the century, art and literature in Great Britain assimilated most of the new ideas and emotions linked to the Romantic movement. However, in France, many concepts began to be questioned after 1789, despite France's more traditional structure of a complex artistic world, and more young French artists during this period began to propose significant changes to the traditional teachings they received.

The Figure of David

David was a very highly regarded artist whose first experiences in Paris were the painting of mythological and historical themes that revealed a deep emotional sensibility.

In 1775, having been awarded the Prix de Rome, he moved to Rome, staying in the area of Emilia Romagna, where he became interested in the Bolognese School of painting, from the Carracci family to Guido Reni. His stay in the city led him to develop a new artistic direction in his work, undertaking a profound revision of Renaissance style classicism, represented by the paintings of Raphael and Nicolas Poussin, at a time in which the new theories of Johann Joachim Winckelmann (1717–1768) and Anton Raphael Mengs (1728–1779) were being established. Nevertheless, it was the study of ancient sculpture that opened up new pictorial perspectives for him.

For many artists he was the indisputable master, although the younger generation of his students inevitably began to modify his teachings.

David's emblematic canvas, *The Oath of the Horatii* (1784), is considered a manifestation of the new classicism because of its compositional rigor, the synthesis of its design, and the solemn eloquence of its language, which is inspired by the atmosphere in the city of Rome.

Jacques-Louis David. The Oath of the Horatii *(1784).*
Oil on canvas, 164.25 × 130 in. The Louvre, Paris.

Jean Broc. The Death of Hyacinth *(1801).*
Oil on canvas, 48.75 × 69 in.
Museum of Fine Arts, Poitiers.

Girodet-Trioson. Portrait of Jean-Baptiste
Belley, Deputy of San Domingo *(1797).*
Oil on canvas, 44 × 61.75 in.
National Museum of the Chateau of Versailles, Paris.

Constance Charpentier and Jean Broc

Among other masters, one of the many young artists who had studied with David was Constance Charpentier (1767–1849). Her work *Melancholy* is clearly inspired by one of the figures of David's *Horatii*, although the general atmosphere of the painting is clearly different. So instead of a dynamic scene, the artist portrays the representation of a woman with an expression of eternal grief, which is underlined by the presence of the natural objects that also appear in the painting.

Jean Broc (1771–1850) was a member of a rebel group of David's pupils who called themselves *Les Primitifs* and whose artistic argument was to adapt the themes and subject matter of ancient times.

In his work *The Death of Hyacinth*, Broc sets aside the committed patriotic themes taken from Greco-Roman history that had inspired David, and instead chooses to paint the Greek myth of the tragic love of Apollo for the young Hyacinth. In this painting both the lighting and the colors, as well as the line of the figures, break with the pictorial examples of the great master.

The Eccentricity of Girodet-Trioson

David must have been surprised to see how his own students contradicted his aesthetic and moral canons in their paintings. They pursued in depth, instead, other effects in which emotions were highly valued. They did this even in paintings with historical themes and characters, such as many by Girodet-Trioson (Anne-Louis Girodet de Roncy).

With the *Portrait of Jean-Baptiste Belley*, Girodet-Trioson exemplified the Revolution's belief in equality with the representation of a free black man who had been previously a slave and who was sent to the convention of the Revolution as a representative of the French Caribbean colony of St. Dominique, along with a white man and a mulatto woman.

Nevertheless, the allegory painted by Girodet-Trioson for the country house of Napoleon at Malmaison, and titled *The Apotheosis of the French Heroes who Died for the Country during the War for Liberty* is even more based on fantasy. Like his master, the artist's intention was to paint a scene from Napoleonic history that would glorify the first consul, though unlike David, he invented an extreme allegory.

JEAN AUGUSTE DOMINIQUE INGRES

Influenced by the work of Raphael, and master of a sharp and infallible vision that allowed him to capture the beauty of what he was painting like no other artist, Ingres' technique was based on the use of fine strokes. Unlike Eugène Delacroix, he started out painting in the purest academic style. His long stay in Italy did not prevent him, on his return to France, from being considered in official circles as the greatest artist of his country. Ingres used his skills as a portraitist to depict his great sense of reality.

The Second Phase of Neo-Classicism

When Jean Auguste Dominique Ingres was born in 1780, art was highly influenced by Neo-Classicism. Encouraged by his father, a modest sculptor and decorator, he soon demonstrated a notable talent for drawing, and from a young age dedicated himself to copying reproductions of art works that his father collected, in particular the paintings of Raphael, Titian, and Rubens.

After his early studies at the Academy of Toulouse, in 1797 he became a pupil of David in Paris, a city to which he moved to complete his training. During this period he painted various portraits, an undertaking that allowed him to show his pictorial talent without breaking off his study of the classical works of the Louvre, his favorite subject.

In September 1806 he traveled to Italy, a country where he lived for over twenty years, first in Rome, where he was particularly impressed by the Sistine Chapel and the Vatican murals, and then in Florence.

The Italian Period

In Rome, Ingres became a portraitist of French subjects, and received official commissions for his works *Bonaparte as First Consul* and *Napoleon I on the Imperial Throne*. He sent some of these works to the Paris salons, but they were heavily criticized, even by Jacques-Louis David himself, who considered them to be too rigid.

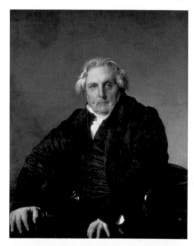

Jean Auguste Dominique Ingres. Portrait of Louis-Francois Bertin (1832). Oil on canvas, 45.5 × 37.5 in. The Louvre, Paris.

Jean Auguste Dominique Ingres. Jupiter and Thetis (1811). Oil on canvas, 101.25 × 130.25 in. Granat-Palais de Malte Museum, Aix-en-Provence.

Jean Auguste Dominique Ingres. Roger Freeing Angelica *(1819). Oil on canvas, 74.75 × 58 in. The Louvre, Paris.*

At the end of his stay at the Villa Médicis, Ingres decided to stay on in Rome, which had become one of the most brilliant cosmopolitan centers of the period.

In 1819 he met up with his friend Bertolini in Florence, a city to which he had now decided to move. Many of his studies of Tuscan painters of the fifteenth and sixteenth centuries have survived from his artistic activity during this period.

Return to France

Elected a member of the Academy on his return to Paris, he opened a studio that was extremely successful. From this time on, apart from the period when he returned to Rome as director of the French Academy (1835–1841) and from which the main works are *Odalisque with Slave* and *Antiochus and Stratonice* are dated, his prestige within official circles grew rapidly.

Ingres' art has always been seen as a contrast to the more passionate work of Eugène Delacroix, too little value being placed on the arduous task of refining his eclecticism within a single style.

THE ARTIST'S LIFE

1780 Born in Montauban (France).

1791 Enters the Toulouse Academy to study painting with Roques and the sculptor Vigan.

1797 Moves to Paris, where he attends the studio of David.

1800 Wins second prize in a competition for the *School of Rome*.

1801 Wins the Rome Prize with his work *Envoys of Agamemnon*.

1802 Participates in the Salon with his first female portrait.

1806 Travels to Rome, making a brief stop in Florence to study Masaccio.

1812 Collaborates in work on the decoration of the Palazzo del Monte Cavallo.

1819 Moves to Florence, where he decides to live, and receives his first official commission from the new French government.

1824 His work *The Vow* receives a triumphant reception at the Salon. Returns to Paris and sets up an *atelier*. One of his pupils is Théodore Chásserieu.

1826 Receives a commission to decorate a new room in the Louvre.

1833 Is named vice-president and soon afterwards president of the School of Fine Arts.

1834 Following criticisms of one of his works, he accepts the post of director of the French Academy in Rome.

1841 Returns to Paris, where he is received triumphantly.

1862 Elected a senator as a form of public recognition.

1867 Dies in Paris.

THÉODORE GÉRICAULT

Considered the great revolutionary of the artistic legacy of Jacques-Louis David, Théodore Géricault was an artist whose career began under the Neo-Classical influence of his master Pierre-Narcisse Guérin, as well as of painters such as Titian and Rembrandt. He copied their works in the Louvre which provided him with a very firm base on which to create large scale figurative and landscape composition. When the Napoleonic era began to decline, along with the loss of his ideals, he began a new period of pictorial investigation.

In Search of New Themes

Théodore Géricault. Enseigne de Maréchal-Ferrant (1814). Oil on board, 48.75 × 40.25 in. Kunstgaus, Zurich.

Born in Rouen, France but living in Paris, Géricault was close to the liberal atmosphere of the old Jacobites and the Napoleonists who met in Guérin's studio. However, the eclipse of Napoleon led to a social change that made it necessary to search for new themes in which, instead of the traditional, legendary heroes, anonymous, everyday people were the main protagonists.

During his stay in Italy (1816–1817), Géricault studied Raphael, Michelangelo, Caravaggio, and the Mannerist painters, as well as Greco-Roman sculpture. This allowed him to depict the Classical and populist world of Rome, a city in which he had diverse experiences of daily life, in an entirely new way and with a great pictorial freedom.

His direct contact with daily life led him to try to depict different themes with great drama, painting large-scale canvases that could compete with those of the Salons and which led him to paint some of his most ambitious works.

Théodore Géricault. Racecourse at Epsom (1821). Oil on canvas, 48.25 × 36.25 in. The Louvre, Paris.

Théodore Géricault. The Raft of the Medusa *(1819). Oil on canvas, 282 × 193.25 in. The Louvre, Paris.*

A Historical Tragedy

The ability to transform a contemporary event into an epic metaphor explains the importance of *The Raft of the Medusa*, a painting that makes reference to a tragic shipwreck that took place in 1816. Géricault prepared the large canvas by painting numerous sketches and notes, until finally he decided to depict the moment when the survivors catch sight of the brigantine *The Argus* and desperately try to attract its attention. Despite the drama reflected in the group of men in the painting, there is a certain relief in the scene because of the remote hope of salvation.

The allegorical message of the painting allows many different interpretations to be made, from considering it to be a symbol of France being dragged along towards the uncertainty of political conservatism to being a universal symbol of human misery.

The London Period

From around 1820 to 1821, Géricault spent more than two years in Great Britain with an exhibition of his paintings. There he found a highly daring alternative to the French tradition of painting in the work of local painters, such as the Scot David Wilkie.

It was during this period that Théodore Géricault began to express in his paintings the more hidden side of the then fascinating city of London, with its ubiquitous filth and poverty.

THE ARTIST'S LIFE

1791 Born in Rouen, France.

1798 Moves with his family to Paris.

1808–1810 Attends the studio of Horace Vernet.

1816–1817 Travels to Italy to study the great masters.

1817 Returns to France, where he meets Eugène Delacroix.

1820–1821 The exhibition of *The Raft of the Medusa* in London and Dublin is a great commercial success.

1821 Publishes a series of lithographs in which he depicts the conditions of misery in London.

1821 Returns to Paris.

1822–1823 In the final years of his active life, he decides to depict mental illness.

1824 Dies in January, not yet thirty-three years old, a few months before the arrival of Francisco de Goya in France.

EUGÈNE DELACROIX

Along with Victor Hugo and Héctor Berlioz, his contemporaries in the fields of literature and music, Eugène Delacroix is considered the great master of the Romantic period. The great authority with which he practiced his profession made him, if not the artist who did most to continue the tradition of Géricault, then at least one of the greatest who did so. He had been a friend of Géricault and posed for *The Raft of the Medusa*. Delacroix's *Diary*, an immensely fascinating literary work, illustrates a precise image of his critical conscience, his modern sensuality, and his curiosity.

Early Works

A member of the upper bourgeois, Eugène Delacroix, like Géricault, attended the studio of Pierre-Narcisse Guérin. Here he received an artistic training that included as an important element studying the works of Michelangelo and Rubens. He was also interested in the techniques of watercolor painting with which he experimented in those years, inspired by Richard Parkes Bonington, and finally in engraving, where he followed the example of Thomas Rowlandson.

The Importance of the *Massacre at Chios*

For the whole of liberal Europe, the Greek rebellion against the Turks was a matter of great interest. In 1824, to repel the Greeks once more, the sultan sent an army com-

Eugène Delacroix. The Barque of Dante (Dante and Virgil in Hell) (1822). Oil on canvas, 96.75 × 74.5 in. The Louvre, Paris.

THE ARTIST'S LIFE

1798 Born in Charenton-Saint-Maurice.

1822 Presents *The Barque of Dante (Dante and Virgil in Hell)* at the Salon, a work that generated argument due to its subject and its compositional drama.

1824 His work *Massacre at Chios* arouses a lot of interest.

1827 With *The Death of Sardanapal*, he demonstrates the character istics of his first period of activity.

1830 *Liberty Leading the People* reveals his involvement in the revolutionary events of the period.

1832 Travels to Morocco, where he begins the second stage of his artistic activity. From Tangiers, he travels to Seville.

1833–1838 Paints the decoration of the *Allegories* for the king's chamber in the Bourbon palace in Paris.

1834 Presents *Women of*

Algiers at the Salon, a work that expresses his fascination for sensual details of the exotic world.

1840 The subject matter of his work returns to the ancient world.

1849–1851 Paints the Chapel of Saint-Anges in Saint-Sulpice.

1850–1851 Paints the decoration for the ceiling of the Apollo Gallery at the Louvre.

1863 Dies in Paris.

Eugène Delacroix. The Death of Sardanapal (1827). Oil on canvas, 195.25 × 154.25 in. The Louvre, Paris.

posed of ten thousand men to the island of Chios, where some twenty thousand inhabitants were murdered, while women and children were turned into slaves to be sold in the markets of North Africa.

In academic circles the painter was criticized for his use of a brilliant chromatic palette, his expressive freedom, and his predilection for exotic literary themes, all elements that made his painting a veritable example of Romantic painting. In 1825 he painted a series of *Odalisques*, although the work that best conveys this spirit is *The Death of Sardanapal*. The subject of the painting, the king of Ninevah who decided to die along with his concubines, horses, and favorite dogs, is a pretext for a canvas full of vibrant rhythms.

Revolutionary Idealism and the Moroccan Period

Although his political and social tendencies were more aristocratic than proletarian, Delacroix witnessed first hand the popular uprisings in Paris on the 27th, 28th, and 29th of July 1830, and decided to commemorate them with his work *Liberty Leading the People (28th of July 1830)*.

In 1832, searching for new sources of inspiration, he made a journey to Morocco, as a guest of the Count of Mornay. His mission was to illustrate the Count's diplomatic posting, which he did with great skill, the result being seven notebooks full of drawings and watercolors that he would later use for inspiration for works like *Women of Algiers*.

Eugène Delacroix. Liberty Leading the People (28th of July 1830) (1830). Oil on canvas, 128 × 102.25 in. The Louvre, Paris.

THE PARIS SALONS FROM 1824–1827

The Salon was the name given to the most important exhibition of French art held at varying intervals from the eighteenth century onward. It was organized under the auspices of the Academy and later controlled by the professors at the School of Fine Arts, who sat on the jury that decided which artists to admit. Despite being controlled by the academic establishment, this did not prevent the eruption of various famous polemics over the rejection of certain artists, among the most famous of whom were the group of Impressionists.

The Salon of 1824

In the Salon of 1824 several new tendencies, both French and foreign, were represented which, for the first time, dealt freely with certain historical themes in their paintings. Thus not only was there a particularly varied section of British watercolor and oil painting, including three works by John Constable, but the exhibition also included, for example, *The Vow of Louis XIII*, the new, transcendental work of Jean Auguste Dominique Ingres.

In this work, King Louis XIII is depicted putting France under the protection of the Virgin of the Ascension in February 1638, a subject that was in itself an evocation of a lost period of history and which the authorities of the Bourbon Restoration wanted to reawaken. Ingres resolved this fusion of Church and State by representing the scene in two parts, highlighting in the lower part the Bourbon king offering his crown and scepter to the Virgin who is holding the baby Jesus in her arms in the upper part.

Because of the painting's intrinsic artistic values, its exhibition at the same time as Eugène Delacroix's *Massacre at Chios* practically consecrated Ingres as the head of the most rebellious young artists, who included Théodore Géricault and Delacroix himself.

New Pictorial Values

For many of the young artists of 1824, the themes in David's paintings were already anachronistic. This was the case among the artists who exhibited at the Salon of Louis Daguerre (1787–1851), whose painting, *Ruins of Holyrood Chapel*, depicts the site of royal Scottish tombs where the two weddings of the disgraced Mary Stuart had been held.

Following in the tradition of the Neo-Dutch domestic scenes of Marguerite Gérard (*Bad News*, exhibited at the Salon of 1804), Constant Debordes (1761–1827), another painter at the Salon, combined a calm language in depicting the homey virtues of looking after children with the triumph of modern medicine in fighting smallpox in his painting, *The Vaccination*. This scene represented a major departure from the previously mentioned works by Ingres and Delacroix.

Jean Auguste Dominique Ingres. The Vow of Louis XIII (1824). Oil on canvas, 106.25 × 134.5 in. Montauban Cathedral.

Eugène Delacroix. Massacre of Chios *(1824).*
Oil on canvas, 139.5 × 165 in. The Louvre, Paris.

The Salon of 1827

What really attracted the public was, in reality, the non-conventional, as was the case at the Salon of 1827, in which the young French rebels, named the Romantics, set about freeing their painting from the outmoded rules of the Academy. Noteworthy among them was Louis Boulanger (1806–1867) with his work *Mazeppa*, based on a tale from Polish legend about the page boy of the same name. This particular work was filled with sadism and sexuality.

The work of the Dutch artist Ary Scheffer entitled *Souliot Women* represented another novelty. Based on the Greek war of independence, Scheffer represented an extreme scene in which a group of women decide to commit mass suicide by throwing themselves off a precipice in order to atone for a collective disgrace.

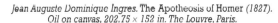

Jean Auguste Dominique Ingres. The Apotheosis of Homer *(1827).*
Oil on canvas, 202.75 × 152 in. The Louvre, Paris.

THE SUCCESSORS TO THE PAINTING OF EUGÈNE DELACROIX

The importance of Delacroix's work influenced numerous artists whose paintings contributed to the creation of a school inspired by the techniques and themes of the master. This group of artists included Théodore Chassériau, who, despite his classical training as a pupil of Jean Auguste Dominique Ingres can be considered, because of his sensual sentimentalism, a member of the group of French Romantic painters from the moment when, in his expansive decorative style and colorist sensuality, he chose to emulate Delacroix more closely.

The School of Delacroix

Delacroix's eagerness to synthesize in his work the conflict between color and design, as well as his predilection for exotic scenes, was not forgotten with the passage of time. The work of many important followers bears witness to the influence of his painting. Among these stands out the painter and lithograph artist Alexandre Gabriel Decamps (1803–1860), who made a trip to Constantinople and Asia Minor in 1827, in other words before Delacroix visited Morocco. Thus he was the author of excellent exotically

inspired paintings such as *Route of Smyrna* and historic paintings such as *The Defeat of the Cimbrians* (1833).

His preference for reality, which is reflected above all in works with less compromising subject matter, converted him, in some respects, into the precursor of Jean François Millet and Gustave Courbet.

Eugène Fromentin and Adolphe Monticelli

Another specialist in painting the Oriental court was the writer, painter, and art critic Eugène Fromentin (1820–1876).

His Romantic background, evident in his paintings of Oriental landscapes and in his writings inspired by his visits to Algeria, made him indifferent to the growing revolution of Impressionism.

Adolphe Monticelli (1824–1886) studied in Paris with Paul Delaroche and copied the grand masters in the Louvre, including painters like Titian, Veronese, Watteau and, of course, Delacroix.

His painting is characterized by noble and rural scenes in vague, Romantic landscapes, using rich color (*Return from the Hunt*, 1885). He also painted still-life, historical, and fantastic compositions, landscapes, and portraits, the latter two genres revealing his great pictorial skill (*Portrait of Madame René*, 1871).

The Work of Chassériau

Théodore Chassériau, the son of a French consul in Santo Domingo and a Creole, began his artistic career at the age of ten. At a young age he moved to Paris, where he was a student of Ingres until 1834, although later his painting moved toward a Romantic form of exoticism.

After Delacroix, he was the most important figurative painter of the period of French Romanticism. Inspired by the sketches and notes he had made during a trip to Algeria, in 1846 he painted famous works that

Alexandre Gabriel Decamps. Turkish Merchant Smoking in his Shop (1844). Oil on canvas, 11 × 14.25 in. The Louvre, Paris.

emulated the colorist sensuality of Delacroix.

An eclectic artist, it is worth mentioning the importance of Ingres' teaching, evident in works such as *Two Sisters* (1843), but so too is the independence with which he stands up for himself next to the great master.

The Feminine Image in *Toilet of Esther*

A work of emotive sensuality in its gentle gestures, *Toilet of Esther* (1842) is one of a series of works in which the painter shows his precocious genius by creating a new type of female image, both strange and disquieting, and hitherto unseen in French painting.

In this painting, the beauty of the form and line come from his master Ingres, which conform to the norms of the most traditional Classicism. At the same time one can also appreciate the unarguably Romantic influence of Delacroix. Although many people consider Ingres and Delacroix to be visual opposites, Chassériau manages to combine his interpretation of the teachings of both masters in this painting.

Théodore Chassériau. Toilet of Esther (1842). Oil on canvas, 14 × 18 in. The Louvre, Paris.

Other Painters

In between Ingres and Delacroix are the works of Victor-Louis Mottez (1809–1897) and the painter Thomas Couture (1815–1879). The latter's works follow the teaching of Tiepolo and the Venetian painters.

Théodore Chassériau. Tepidarium of Pompey (1853). Oil on canvas, 10.5 × 67.25 in. Musée d'Orsay, Paris.

THE EIGHTEENTH CENTURY AND CLASSICISM

The leading figures of Classicism in France were David, Gérard, Gros, Prud'hon and Ingres. In Germany, two artists of opposing artistic tendencies who heralded the beginning of German Classicism were Anton Raphael Mengs and Asmus Jakob Carstens. Their work, however, lacks the degree of perfection and completeness that characterize the paintings by French artists such as David.

The Paintings and Theory of Mengs

Anton Raphael Mengs (1728–1779) was the first Classical painter in Germany. An artist inclined toward the theoretical, he was introduced to the world of art by his father Ismael, a painter and miniaturist in the Dresden court of Augustus III of Saxony. In 1741, Mengs went to Rome to complete his training, which included the study of Roman antiquity and paintings by the great Italian masters, in particular Raphael. His friendship with Johann Joachim Winckelmann in Rome, his connection with the world of Roman antiquities, his discovery of Herculaneum (1736) and Pompeii (1748) were instrumental in his becoming an important leader in determining the direction of the Neo-Classical movement.

In 1754 Mengs was named director of the Capitoline Academy in Rome, a position from which he disseminated his new artistic ideals. These ideals are embodied in *Parnassus*, a work he painted on the dome of the Villa Albani gallery that he completed in 1761.

The large frescoes in the royal palaces of Madrid and Aranjuez, Mengs' monumental paintings of his later years, are examples of how the artist combined academic and eclectic styles within a fanciful baroque framework. Mengs was renowned among his contemporaries for the highly desired portraits he painted for his high-society patrons in almost all of the courts in Europe.

The Ancient World in Carstens

Asmus Jakob Carstens (1754–1798) was known in the world of art as a rebellious and solitary character. A Dane of German origin, Carstens was virtually a self-taught painter.

Carstens settled in Rome in 1792, thanks primarily to a grant he received from the Prussian government. There he came into contact with German artists living in the city. His friendship with Bertel Thorvaldsen led him to the study of works of antiquity and the

Anton Raphael Mengs.
Prince Charles IV.
Oil on canvas, 43.25 × 59.75 in.
The Prado, Madrid.

Anton Raphael Mengs. Self-portrait. Oil on canvas, 20 × 24.75 in. The Prado, Madrid.

The Spread of Classicism in Germany

After 1750, German art did not undergo a revolution in the same way that French art did. However, following Carsten's example, there were some traces of Romanticism in the works of artists such as Eberhard Wächter (1762–1852), Joseph Anton Koch (1768–1839), and Peter Cornelius (1783–1867) among others.

There is little evidence of innovation among the artists from this period of transition. And where innovation does exist, it is accompanied by traditional forms of expression.

The art of portrait painting, however, did gain importance in Germany toward the end of the eighteenth century. This was especially true for the works of artists such as J.G. Ziesenis (1716–1776), a court painter for various German courts; Anton Graff (1736–1813), a Swiss artist who spent most of his life in Dresden; and Johann Friedrich August Tischbein (1750–1812), who lived most of his life in Italy and France.

Renaissance, where he succumbed to the influence of Raphael and Michelangelo.

Rejecting the precepts of the Academy, he went on to develop a style of art that was based on quick composition dictated solely by internal laws. This approach was in contrast to the work of his contemporaries, which was based on reason and technical dexterity.

Mengs' rhetoric is opposed to that of Carstens, whose artistic trajectory is fragmented because of a large number of unfinished works. Thus, Mengs' most important works, which were done while he was in Rome, are primarily sketches he did for large murals based on themes from Greek mythology. His many drawings demonstrate that it was Mengs, more than any other artist of the period, who was best able to reproduce Winckelmann's attitude toward Greek antiquity.

Asmus Jakob Carstens. Fight between Fingal and the Spirit of Loda (after 1796). Oil on canvas, 39.5 × 31 in. Statens Museum for Kunst, Copenhagen.

CASPAR DAVID FRIEDRICH

Romanticism as an ideal was not an exclusively French phenomenon. Another focal point was Germany in the late eighteenth century, which also chose to extol both individuality and the past. In painting, however, artistic interpretation varied, but works based on what was truly Romantic predominated. In this regard, the figure of Caspar David Friedrich stands out as the most noted representative of German landscape painting.

Friedrich's Art and Forms

Friedrich's painting underwent very few changes over the course of its evolution. The subject matter of his work reflected the different stages of his artistic career and the different places where he lived. After completing his studies at the Academy of Copenhagen, he moved to Dresden, a city that at that time was the center of Romanticism. Except for brief visits to the town where he was born, Friedrich lived almost uninterruptedly in Dresden and quickly immersed himself in the atmosphere of Romantic culture, in the company of Friedrich Leopold von Hardenberg (Novalis), Ludwig Tieck and, later, Johann Wolfgang von Goethe. The main themes of his paintings were the shores of the Baltic Sea, the port of Greifswald, the ruins of the gothic monastery at Eldena, Dresden and its surroundings, and the Harz Mountains, all places where he painted the phenomena of nature, such as the mist on the seashore, arid fields, banks of clouds at dusk in a sky illuminated by a splendid sunset, dusk on the mountain top, and so on.

Friedrich's paintings are considered depictions of a spiritualized nature, typical of Romanticism.

Caspar David Friedrich. **Abbey in the Oakwood** *(1809–1810). Oil on canvas, 67.25 × 44 in. Schloss Charlottenburg, Berlin.*

Caspar David Friedrich. Stages of Life *(1834–1835). Oil on canvas, 37 × 28.75 in. Museum der bildenden Künste, Leipzig.*

Man Before an Immense Landscape

In Friedrich's paintings, the smallness of the figures in the landscape takes on, for the first time, a greater significance than in any previous era. In many of the paintings, the figures might be seen from behind, as they contemplate a moon-lit landscape, or at a window. These depictions are expressions of the Romantic desire to embrace the universe proclaimed by Novalis, who said that "an individual's soul should be in harmony with the universal soul."

Friedrich preferred the landscape at certain times of the day, in the morning or the afternoon, at the time when it was best to establish the psychological correlations in which to place the small human figures. A certain ascetic quality can be seen in *Monk by the Sea* (1809–1810).

Other Works

With the painting *Abbey in the Oakwood* (1809–1810), Friedrich offered a greater number of narrative and landscape components. Thus, through the sepia-colored mist and against the black silhouettes of the leafless trees and ruins of a gothic abbey,

Caspar David Friedrich. The White Cliffs of Rugen.
Oil on canvas, 67.25 × 44 in.
Oskar Reinhardt Collection, Winterthur.

one discerns a procession of monks advancing through a snow-covered cemetery carrying a coffin toward the roofless nave. Though he was an artist who never created a real school, the output of the artists who worked around Friedrich is interesting. Among these artists were Carl Gustav Carus, August Heinrich, Johan Christian Dahl, and Georg Friedrich Kersting.

THE ARTIST'S LIFE

1774 Born in Griefswald, Pomerania, a port on the Baltic Sea.

1794–1798 Studies at the Academy in Copenhagen.

1798 Moves to Dresden, where he did most of his work.

1807 His work *Dolmen in the Snow* reveals a sense of tremendous panic toward nature.

1808 Paints *The Cross in the Mountains*, which raises controversy because of the bold representations of religious and symbolic elements in the landscape.

1810 Gains recognition for his work for the first time with works such as *Abbey in the Oakwood*, exhibited at the Academy in Berlin. Dedicates himself to teaching. Begins a period of progressive isolation.

1818 His work *Wanderer before a Sea of Fog* shows the importance of man in the splendor of nature.

1840 Dies in Dresden poverty stricken and in deep melancholy.

FRIEDRICH'S SUCCESSORS

Although quickly forgotten, Caspar David Friedrich's art was revived by his imitators, particularly in some of its philosophical, religious, or poetic aspects. Furthermore, those who had had direct contact with the artist realized that his technique could show them a way toward evolving their own art. Therefore by using various elements of the more typical aspects of the master's work, some of them achieved a certain degree of fame, while for others he provided a starting point.

The Landscapes of Carus and Heinrich

Carl Gustav Carus (1789–1869) was one of the painters closest to Friedrich in his conception of nature and subject matter. His half-artistic, half-scientific mode of perception shows the influence of Geothe. In some works, such as his depiction of an artist's empty studio (*Easel in Moonlight*), he managed to free himself from Friedrich's influence. In general one can say that his canvases reflect those of an art lover who expresses Romantic elements in a pleasant way.

August Heinrich (1794–1822), a follower of Friedrich, worked in the same circle as Friedrich and Johan Christian Clausen Dahl. He lived in Vienna, Salzburg, and Innsbruck, and shared with his master a concern for the small details in a landscape that give life to a painting. Heinrich's work also shows influence of

Georg Friedrich Kersting. Young Woman Sewing by Lamp Light (1828). Oil on canvas, 13.5 × 16 in. Neue Pinakothek, Munich.

the Nazarene landscape artists, with whom he came into contact during his stay in Austria. An artist more closely associated with Friedrich was Ernest Ferdinand Oehme (1797–1855), who spent an extended period of time in Italy (1819–1825) and connected with the Nazarenes in Rome. His work, which at first was highly suggestive of the Romantic ideals of his master (for example, *Cathedral in Winter*, 1821), reflected Dahl's melancholic landscape and, in particular, the rich descriptive detail of his friend Adrian Ludwig Richter.

Carl Gustav Carus. Inning Cemetery (c. 1822). Oil on canvas, 11.25 × 8.5 in. Neue Pinakothek, Munich.

Dahl's Contribution

Norwegian by birth, although from 1818 onward he spent the larger part of his life in Dresden, Johan Christian Clausen Dahl was the first and most important painter of Norwegian landscape. Although, like Friedrich, he gave great importance to, and focused on, manifestations of light and atmosphere, he cannot be considered to have painted in the same view as Friedrich, despite the impression that his work gives.

For Friedrich, light and atmosphere were factors that, to put it a certain way, constituted the soul of the landscape. For Dahl these were phenomena in themselves, and with his studio he founded the naturalist landscape painting, revealing his singular sensibility in depicting atmosphere.

Nevertheless, without Friedrich's representations of immense landscapes, the studies of sky and clouds that Dahl painted would not have occurred. They represented a new departure because of their way of including in the painting a thin strip of land, a copse of trees or two, or some element linked to the presence of man (*Study of Clouds*, c. 1825).

Johan Christian Clausen Dahl.
Winter in Sognfjord *(1827)*

The Work of Kersting

Georg Friedrich Kersting was a close friend of Friedrich, of whom he painted two portraits in 1819 standing in front of his easel in an extremely cold studio. He was an artist, although not a landscape painter, who belonged to the first generation of German Romantic painters. These artists recreated themes linked to the sentimental emotions in literature of the period, attempting to express a national art that was closely tied to the patriotic enthusiasm that had arisen as a result of the Napoleonic invasion.

From 1805 to 1808 he studied at the Academy of Copenhagen, and from then until 1819 lived in Dresden. In that year he was nominated director of the painting department of the famous Meissen porcelain factory.

His best artistic achievements were those in which he represented the daily life of the German petit bourgeoisie by means of an exact and meticulous description of their surroundings and their most pertinent belongings

Johan Christian Clausen Dahl.
The Day after a Stormy Night *(1819).*
Oil on canvas, 41.5 × 29.25 in.
Neue Pinakothek, Munich.

PHILIPP OTTO RUNGE

Famous for his theories about the essence of painting, Philipp Otto Runge's work
is considered to be the incarnation of Romanticism in Germany. He was one of
those artists who were ambitious to find a completely new symbolic language
for art, nature, and religion and who, like William Blake, felt destined to
revive a civilization that was on its death bed. Thus his artistic legacy constitutes
a summary of his efforts to rejuvenate the religious traditions of the West.

Runge's Theory

Philipp Otto Runge began his studies in Hamburg, but soon afterward attended the academies of Copenhagen and Dresden. In this latter city he established contact with a circle of Romantic painters and poets and in 1803 visited Goethe in Weimar. From then on he maintained a frequent correspondence with the writer, which dealt above all with the problem of color. Together with Friedrich, he is considered the founder of German Romantic painting, not so much for the few

*Philipp Otto Runge.
Self-portrait.
Kunsthalle, Hamburg.*

paintings he produced, but for his theories on the nature of painting.

He painted the daily activity of the people and places he knew in Hamburg and its surroundings. This is reflected in some of the portraits he painted, such as the ones he made between 1805 and 1806 of the three children of Friedrich August Hülsenbeck, a friend of his brother Daniel.

Stylistically, through the influence of Asmus Jakob Carstens and John Flaxman, he remained tied to the Classical taste for line in spite of his later theoretical studies on the elemental effects of color and its symbolic and psychological significance (*The Sphere of Colors*, 1810). This is evident from his drawings and his extremely fine engravings.

*Philipp Otto Runge.
Morning (1808).
Oil on canvas, 33 × 42 in.
Kunsthalle, Hamburg.*

Allegorical Imagery

Runge made constant studies of the esoteric Romanticism of contemporary poets like Wackenroder, Novalis, Holderlin, and especially Tieck. Thus mysticism is evident in a series entitled *The Four Stages of the Day* which, according to Runge was to be an "abstract, pictorial, fantastic musical poem." He intended it to become a natural cycle in four parts that would not only evoke, by means of allegorical landscape and characters, the moments of the day and the four seasons, but would also include an allusive series of Christian, humanist, and even political symbols. An impression of the whole is given in *Morning* (1808), in which the rigorous symmetry and marginal images create a composition that, like the work of Blake, refers to the mystical world of the Middle Ages, one of holy worship and the spirit.

Color and Light

In his desire for totality, Runge involved himself in the problem of light and color. His attempts to achieve the representation of both light and color in the most perfect form possible led the artist to study the elemental effects of color and particularly their symbolic values, as can be seen in his theoretical work *Farbkugel*.

Philipp Otto Runge. The Parents and Children of the Artist *(1806). Kunsthalle, Hamburg.*

He studied the properties and laws of chromatic relationships with scientific, psychological, and mystical speculations, and in this sense can be considered the precursor of the theoreticians and painters of the post-Impressionist period. In his portraits, Runge occasionally made use of an arcane light, in this way turning his work into a form of poetic painting but retaining, elsewhere, a balance between objectivity and Romanticism (*The Artist's Parents*, 1806).

THE ARTIST'S LIFE

1777 Born in Wolgast, the old Swiss Pomerania. Headed for a career in commerce, he does not devote himself to painting until he is twenty.

1799–1801 Studies at the Academy of Copenhagen with the Classicists Nicolai Abraham Abildgaard and Jens Juel.

1801 Meets Caspar David Friedrich in Greifswald.

1801–1803 Studies with Anton Graff at the Academy of Dresden, a city where he meets Romantic painters and poets.

1803 In Weimar meets Johann Wolfgang von Goethe, with whom he begins a private correspondence based on the treatment of color.

1803–1810 Moves to Hamburg, where he is looked after by his brother. His later work is linked to a Romanticism of an esoteric nature.

1810 Dies in Hamburg.

THE GROUP OF THE NAZARENES

The generation of artists that followed Caspar David Friedrich and Phillip Otto Runge
were that of the Nazarenes, a group of German painters characterized by their opposition
to the Classicist Academic approach and by their search for an ideal of religious life.
They took as their model the old masters of German Medieval art, up to Dürer, and the
Italian painting of the *Quattrocento*, including Raphael. Nazarene art had a notable
influence on German painting in the nineteenth century.

Northern European and Mediterranean Traditions

Like writers, German artists
began to concentrate on the
Classical traditions of the
Mediterranean and Northern
Europe on the one hand, and on
the main traditions of the West
on the other. The latter traditions were more spiritual and
had reached their most splendid expression in the Gothic
cathedral, the symbolic incarnation of a society and its art
united in the Christian faith.
This was now seen as a possible source of inspiration for
the reform of both art and life in
the nineteenth century. In this
context, the prescient state-
ment made by Goethe in an
essay of 1773 on Gothic architecture and the Germanic spirit
was eventually taken up by
Friedrich Schlegel.

Wilhelm von Schadow. Joseph Interpreting Dreams *(1812).
12.25 × 13.75 in. Neue Pinakothek, Munich.*

The Renaissance in Christian Art

The Nazarenes' intention
was to bring about a renaissance in Christian art by following a belief, more or less clearly
stated, that focused on the religious painting of the two artistic
periods mentioned above.

Their intention of forming a
group of collaborators with a
common agenda was nothing
more than a return to the
communities of the Medieval
period, and thus, in July 1809,
they formed their group at the
Academy of Vienna.

Guided by Friedrich Over-
beck and Franz Pforr (1788–
1812) in the Community of

Saint Lucas, their principal
members were Joseph Winter-
gerst (1783–1867), Joseph Sutter
de Linz (1781–1866), the Swiss
artists Georg Ludwig Voget
(1788–1879), and Johann Konrad
Hottinger (1788–1828).

Before the end of 1809 the
community moved to Rome and
established itself in the abandoned convent of Saint Isidorus
in the Pincio, which had been
closed down by Napoleon, and
they converted themselves into
monks in a monastery of art.

With time, other German
painters joined the group, such
as Peter Cornelius, Julius

Schnorr von Carolsfeld (1794–
1872), Friedrich Olivier (1791–
1859), the Veit brothers Johan-
nes and Phillip, Wilhelm von
Schadow (1788–1862), the Viennese artist Johann Evangelist
Scheffer von Leonhardsoff (1795–
1822), and Joseph Führich
(1800–1876) from Bohemia.

The Ideals of Primitive Art Among the Nazarenes

The religious element that
united these artists led, in the
case of some of them, to a
return to the grandiose forms

of the Italian *Quattrocento* in the work of painters like Perugino, Beato Angelico, Lucas Signorelli, and Filippo Lippi, as well as Raphael, the great model for the classicists. Other artists found their models, on the other hand, in ancient German painting and in Dürer.

The religious element was the main theme of the Nazarenes' painting, and was the only element that classifies their art as Romantic. For a long time the spiritual content of this painting was restricted to religious narrative, although it could never be compared with Medieval painting.

Nevertheless, religion was not the only theme depicted by the Nazarenes. Landscape and portraits, albeit in isolation, complemented their artistic lives.

The Great Elemental Paintings

In 1816–1817, the consul general of Prussia, Jakob

Wilhelm von Schadow. Young Roman Woman (1818). 28.75 × 37 in. Neue Pinakothek, Munich.

Salomon Bartholdy, decided to have a room in the Palazzo Zuccari painted with decorations of scenes from the Old Testament. These frescoes, which are today in the National Gallery of Berlin, were painted by Cornelius, Overbeck, Veit, and Schadow. Some years later, the Marquis Carlo Massimo commissioned paintings for three rooms in his villa near San Giovanni in Laterano (Rome), which were painted by Cornelius, Joseph Anton Koch, and Veit (the Dante room); Schnorr (the Ariosto room); and Overbeck and Führich (the Tasso room).

Friedrich Olivier. Loisach Valley (c. 1842–1845). Oil on canvas, 11.75 × 8 in. Neue Pinakothek, Munich.

ROMANTICISM IN GERMANY

FRANZ PFORR
AND FRIEDRICH OVERBECK

These two painters, both exponents of the Nazarene enthusiasm for primitive
Christian art, met in 1808 studying the — for them — antiquated artistic discipline
that was based on Greco-Roman sculpture and the canons of great art of the
sixteenth and seventeenth centuries of the Academy of Vienna.

The Peculiar Painting
of Franz Pforr

Franz Pforr (1788–1812)
trained in Kassel with Johann
Heinrich Wilhelm Tischbein,
and although he died young, he
revealed himself in Rome to be
one of the most original personalities of the Nazarene movement. He also shared the
artistic interests of artists like
William Blake and John Flaxman
or those of the Primitives of
David's studio.

In addition, his personal
pictorial focus that reflected his
ideals came, to a certain extent,
close to the artistic style of
French troubadours. In his
work entitled *Entry of Rudolf
von Habsburg into Basle in
1273*, begun in Vienna in 1808
and finished in Rome in 1810,
one can identify very clearly in
this Medieval style the Northern European influence.

In this painting Pforr attempted to depict faithfully the
peasantry of the Middle Ages,
although many details, such as
their clothes, are actually anachronistic. The truly important
thing in the painting is the
intense desire to recover and
re-experience a period that
had been definitively lost.

Other Works

Pforr was one of those artists
whose independence of form
in his paintings marked him as
one of the less ascetic tem-
peraments and one of the most
successful artists among the
Nazarenes. His work *Rudolf von
Habsburg and the Priest* (1809)
is also very original. The

figures and the forms of objects,
represented with a minimum of
modeling, characterize a canvas
in which the Medieval theme is
reworked with a decidedly
Romantic Primitivism.

In 1812, the year of his
premature death, Franz Pforr
completed a diptych for Friedrich Overbeck that used allegorical female figures to
represent the disparity between
Italian and European art.

Friedrich Overbeck and
the Leadership of the
Nazarenes

Overbeck attended the art
school of J. Peroux in his home
town of Lubeck, and was highly
influenced by engravings of
the works of Giotto, Simone
Martini, Masaccio, and Perugino
that circulated around Germany in that period. The result
of his friendship and arguments about art with Pforr in
Vienna can be seen in his
canvases of 1808–1809, in

Friedrich Overbeck. Portrait of Pforr in Traditional
German National Costume *(1810). Oil on canvas,
18.5 × 24.5 in. Staatliche Museen Preussischer
Kulturbesitz, National Gallery, Berlin.*

Friedrich Overbeck.
Italia and Germania *(1829).*
Oil on canvas,
41.25 × 37.25 in.
Neue Pinakothek, Munich.

which Medieval and religious themes represent a clear reaction to the Neo-Classical ideas of Winckelmann and Mengs, who were at that time dominant in the field of art.

When he created the Community of Saint Lucas, the hostility of official Viennese circles made him decide to move to Rome. After founding the group of Nazarenes, in 1811 Overbeck began to work on the last idea of Pforr, translated into a historical fantasy entitled *Italia and Germania*, which he did not finish until 1829.

The Great Pictorial Cycles in Rome

Together with Peter Cornelius, Wilhelm von Schadow, and Philipp Veit, Overbeck painted the fresco *Story of Joseph in Egypt*. It was a pictorial cycle that was notably significant for the Romantic movement in Germany. In another collective work, the frescoes for the house of the Marquis Massimo (1819–1830), Overbeck recreated scenes from *Personification of Jerusalem Delivered* (*Olindo and Sofronia, Edward and Gildippe*) characterized by their clean, dry line, as well as their fresh

polychromatic nature. In artistic terms, Overbeck overlapped with the group of Purists.

Taken together, the art of Pforr and Overbeck can be seen as anticipating the principles that the brotherhood of pre-Raphaelites defended and championed as their own and, whose objectives in 1848 would be so similar to the heterogeneous group of the Nazarenes.

Friedrich Overbeck. Vittoria Caldoni da Albano *(1821).*
Oil on canvas, 25.75 × 35 in. Neue Pinakothek, Munich.

PETER CORNELIUS AND OTHER NAZARENE ARTISTS

The numerous painters who constituted the group of Nazarenes left behind many interesting works. The ideal of Primitive art by which they were guided was as heterogeneous as the ideal of the Classicists, and once again turned Rome into a focal point of artistic creation. The Eternal City became the center of activity for any artist who followed in the tradition of ancient German painting.

The Independence of Peter Cornelius

Alongside Franz Pforr and Friedrich Overbeck, Peter Cornelius was considered one of the most influential members of the group of Nazarenes, having met the group in Rome in 1811. However, he was an artist who maintained his independent approach.

He produced drawings, decorative frescoes, biblical and mythical paintings, and other works. From the whole of his work, two items stand out for being different from the rest, twelve drawings to illustrate Goethe's *Faust* and seven drawings for *Niebelungenlied* (1812–1817), which show the influence of Dürer's engravings.

Similar also to the art of Asmus Jakob Carstens, Cornelius' mural painting *The Final Judgment* (1836–1839), in the choir of the Ludwigskirche de Friedrich von Gartner in Munich, is a clear example of his ideology. However, his final work was his most significant, namely the sketches on which he worked from 1843 for a mural painting for a cemetery planned for Berlin, the city where he lived from 1840 onward.

Julius Schnorr and Karl Philipp Fohr

Cornelius painted epic heroes who became a reference for a series of artists of that time, encouraging them to represent the history and legends of their countries, as well as Classical mythology and allegories as themes for murals. In the same vein, the frescoes by Julius Schnorr von Carolsfeld, which depicted the legend of the Nibelung or episodes in the lives of Charlemagne, Redbeard, and Rudolf of Hapsburg in the royal palace of Munich (1831–1842), were made without recourse to architectural forms, as were the murals in the Ariosto room.

Schnorr was an artist who stands out for his series of portraits of friends and Roman patrons. So does Fohr (1795–1818), whose accuracy in the reproduction of the human body and the meticulous depiction of details give a certain feeling of improvisation.

The Olivier Brothers

One of the most important Nazarene artists and landscape painters of the group, Ferdinand Olivier (1785–1841) never went to Italy. He was born in Dessau where, along with his brother Heinrich (1783–1848), he met

Peter Cornelius.
Faust and
Mephistopheles in
Rabestein *(1816).*
*Burin engraving on
vergé paper by
F. Ruschewyh,
20.75 × 16.5 in.
Graphische Sammlung,
Kunstmuseum,
Düsseldorf.*

Julius Schnorr von Carolsfeld. Pictorial mural decoration in the Ariosto room in the house of the Marquis Carlo Massimo in Rome (1823).

Prince Leopold Friedrich Franz de Anhalt-Dessau. In Dresden, between 1804 and 1806, the two brothers were part of the Romantic circle. Later, during a stay in Paris, they painted two religious paintings together, *The Baptism of Christ* and *The Last Supper*, for the chapel of Wörlitz. These were shy, early representations of what would become Nazarene art.

From 1814 to 1816 Ferdinand painted a collection of views of Vienna that show his deep understanding of the world of landscape themes set against the background of a large city. These works were seen as significant and created a school.

Friedrich Olivier

Friedrich Olivier competed with his brother in many ways, but apart from some isolated landscape works, he was very different from him. His ambition was to be more versatile, and consequently he went on to paint various portraits that have been judged magnificent. In some of his drawings one can see a continuation of the work of Dürer, Martin Schongauer, and other late Gothic German artists and, likewise, one can see Olivier's intense assimilation of their artistic examples.

Karl Philipp Fohr. Landscape near Rocca Canterano in the Sabine Hills (1818). Oil on canvas, 53.25 × 38.5 in. Schlossmuseum, Darmstadt.

THE PURIST MOVEMENT

Nazarene art left its mark on Italian painting, particularly on the currents of Purism.
Thus, the Italian Purist movement was created from the experiences of the Nazarenes.
Like them, the Italian Purists advocated religion as an inspiration for art, and
reevaluated the painting of the *Trecento* and *Quattrocento*. Nevertheless, this return to
the past also had Nationalist implications, reawakening the great traditions of Italian
art which, in the eyes of many, had been dormant since the death of Raphael.

The Purist Aesthetic

Taking an ethical sense of art as their reference, Purism recognized a stylistic model in the work of the Primitive artists, from Cimabue to early Raphael, in which simplicity in style and composition were key. The artists who participated in this resurrection of Christian art around the middle of the nineteenth century had no difficulty finding inspiration from numerous sources.

For a Belgian like Antoine Wiertz (1806–1865), it was Rubens who best incarnated the artistic ideal in painting, but for an Italian like Tommaso Minardi (1787–1871), it was easier, or stylistically more fitting, to find an aesthetic and moral beauty in the work of Raphael and even in works of more distant periods.

The reason is simple: For this artist the periods of Italian art that were more ancient and less theoretically corrupt were the best source of aesthetic and religious purity. This was a point of view that in Italy was summed up in a famous text.

The Purist Manifesto

Argument over Purism began in 1833, driven by the painter and writer Antonio Bianchini, a student of Minardi, who used the term Purism to describe something similar to what was happening in the field of language, in which Tuscan literary models from the *Trecento* were being propounded. Bianchini published a manifesto of Purism (*On Purism in the Arts*, 1842) which was signed by Friedrich Overbeck, Minardi

himself, and the sculptor Pietro Tenerari. With this initiative, these artists were convinced that it was possible to renovate art if one rejected the sophisticated creation of illusion and the techniques of chiaroscuro, which they considered decadent, later-day, Western styles. Their initiative promoted a constant trend in the art and aesthetic theory of the nineteenth century.

Purism spread in Rome thanks to Minardi and in Tuscany thanks to Luigi Mussini (1813–

Paul Delaroche.
The Death of Queen
Elizabeth *(1828).*
135 × 166.25 in.
The Louvre, Paris.

Hippolyte-Jean Flandrin. Portrait of Madame Flandrin (1846). 26 × 32.75 in. The Louvre, Paris.

his brother Cesare. In 1830, as a student at the Florence Academy, he was a pupil of Pietro Benvenuti (1769–1844) and Giuseppe Bezzuoli (1784–1855). Already labeled a Purist in 1835, he associated himself with the Nazarene imitation of *umbre* painting of the fifteenth century with his work *Holy Music* (1841). With his move to Paris in 1849, and through direct contact with the work of Ingres, Mussini's style became more sophisticated. The venerated tradition continued to inspire not just the Italians but also other artists who were involved in the resurrection of Christian art, such as the Scottish painter William Dyce (1806–1864). Furthermore, the spirit of the time was favorable to the resurgence of great mural commissions, with two artists standing out, Hippolyte-Jean Flandrin (1809–1864) and Paul Delaroche.

1888). The painters A. Ciseri and C. Brumidi, both students of Minardi, and A. Franchi and A. Cassioli, students of Luigi Mussini, also joined the movement.

Tomasso Minardi

Tomasso Minardi was trained at the Accademia di San Luca in Rome, and became familiar with the painting of Felice Giani (1758–1823) and Vincenzo Camuccini (1771–1844). He later stayed in Milan, where he met G. Rossi and A. Appiani.

With his work entitled *Supper at Emmaus* (1807), he showed his fascination for Venetian and Flemish colorism and for the drawing of the fifteenth century, two factors that characterized all his subsequent activity. In 1825, in his painting, *Saint Stanislav on his Deathbed,* he added to the dispute between Neoclassicists and Nazarenes by identifying with the line and *umbere* (shadow) style painting of the *Quattrocento*.

Luigi Mussini and Other Artists

Luigi Mussini started to paint under the guidance of

Paul Delaroche. Bonaparte Crossing the Alps (1848). 87.5 × 113.75 in. The Louvre, Paris.

CARL SPITZWEG AND BIEDERMEIER ROMANTICISM

The term Biedermeier defines a comfortable, functional style suitable for the demands of the bourgeois society of the time, and was initially applied to the decorative arts in the Germanic countries during the period of the Restoration (1815–1848). Biedermeier brought about the resurgence of a tendency in German Romanticism that is represented by artists who were draftsmen rather than painters.

Between Realism and Idealization

Born in Munich, Carl Spitzweg (1808–1885) did not begin his artistic career until 1833. After a period of self-teaching, he developed a personal style by which he showed his great ability as a painter. He lived in Italy in 1832, and in 1836 began to exhibit his work. His travels to Great Britain and France gave him the opportunity to see firsthand the satirical painting of both countries, as well as to come into contact with French Romanticism. He specialized in genre painting, full of realistic, sarcastic details, which often came from Biedermeier themes.

The two virtues that stand out most in the painter contrast directly with one another, and furthermore constitute a characteristic element of his work: the authenticity of the environment he paints (*The Poor Poet*, 1899) and the charm of the delicate and masterful tonality typical of his landscapes, in which he depicts a world of dreams.

Moritz von Schwind. The Visit (c. 1855). 20 × 28.25 in. Neue Pinakothek, Munich.

Moritz von Schwind and Adrian Ludwig Richter

Following his university education, Moritz von Schwind (1804–1971) became a member of Viennese literary and musical circles. He achieved his greatest artistic success as an illustrator of literary works and a contributor to satirical periodicals. He soon distanced himself from the Italian style of the Nazarenes to focus on the reaffirmation of the German Middle Ages and on Germanic

Carl Spitzweg. The Poor Poet (1899). Neue Pinakothek, Munich.

Adrian Ludwig Richter.
The Watzmann (1824).
36.5 × 47.25 in.
Neue Pinakothek,
Munich.

The Work of Alfred Rethel

Considered another great master of drawing who was active in Germany, Alfred Rethel (1816–1859) cannot qualify as a Biedermeier Romantic, although his engravings reflect that style. He trained at the Academy in Düsseldorf and lived in Italy, Dresden, and Frankfurt, a city where he came into contact with the group of Nazarenes. In 1840 he was commissioned to paint scenes from the life of Charlemagne as frescoes for the Imperial Hall of the Aachen City Hall. This became his most important artistic achievement.

Landscape Painting

popular sagas (*The procession of Kuno von Falkenstem*, 1843–1844), and became the artist who was most representative of the Biedermeier style.

Compared with Schwind's art, Adrian Ludwig Richter's work appears more hetero-geneous. Following a period during which he was influenced by the landscapes of Salzburg and the painting of these by Joseph Anton Koch, Richter specialized in the world of peasants and scenes from the petit-bourgeoisie.

In landscape painting it is difficult to detach oneself from nature, yet the landscape painting of this period acquired a certain bourgeois tone. The works of the period by Carl Rottmann (1797–1850) or Franz Dreber (1822–1875) are some of the genre's best examples.

Carl Rottmann.
Marathon *(1848).*
Wall mural,
78.75 × 61.75.
Neue Pinakothek,
Munich.

THE CLASSIC-ACADEMIC TRADITION

At the end of the eighteenth century, Spain did not undergo any abrupt transformation in its artistic orientation, nor did it expect to. The early years of the nineteenth century saw a continuation of the ideas of the preceding decades and, during the reign of Charles IV, the court leaned in between an Academicism with Classical influences, a period inspired by the French and Italian baroque, and a decorative motif that was close to Rococo.

Academies and Schools of Fine Art

Although the influence of the Academicist current was fairly universal, there was one painter, Francisco de Goya (1746–1828), who was so opposed to all academic guidelines that it is difficult to arbitrarily differentiate his artistic work between the two centuries that correspond to the date of his birth and death.

The popularity of Goya's art was very limited during the life of the painter because of the rigid aesthetic directives concerning the role that art had to fulfil in Spain at the beginning of the century. These directives were completely at variance with the freedom from rules that the brilliant Aragonese artist advocated. At this time, the Academies and Schools of Fine Arts had managed to completely substitute the studios as centers for artistic training and to imbue a utilitarian conception of art and a social conditioning of the artist himself.

Vicente López

Vicente López (1772–1850) represents the final great exponent of the Spanish academic tradition in the eighteenth century. He started his training at the San Carlos Academy in his hometown of Valencia in 1785. His painting *King Ezekial Displaying his Wealth* won the first prize at the Academy in 1789 and enabled him to continue his studies in Madrid.

In the capital he studied sixteenth-century painting, copying Luca Giordano and Claudio Coello, and he came into contact with the academic tradition begun by Mengs, which at that time was represented by Francisco Bayeu and Mariano Salvador Maella. The following year he won first prize in the competition of the Academy of San Fernando with the work *The Catholic Kings Receiving the Ambassador of the King of Fez.*

Vicente López. Francisco de Goya *(1826).*
Oil on canvas, 29.5 × 36.5 in.
The Prado, Madrid.

Vicente López.
Madam Vargas Machuca.
Oil on canvas, 22.75 × 28.75 in.
Romantic Museum, Madrid.

Vicente López.
Paying Homage to
Charles IV and His
Family *(1802).*
Oil on canvas,
98 × 151.25 in.
The Prado, Madrid.

The Valencian Period

In 1792 he moved back to Valencia, where he immediately enjoyed a notable prestige.

As well as being a professor at the Academy of San Carlos, of which he was nominated president in 1801, he painted numerous commissions, mostly of religious paintings and decorative murals for churches in Valencia.

He also produced portraits, projects for monuments, and drawings for engravings. Particularly noteworthy during this period are his paintings that commemorate the visit to Valencia of King Charles IV and his wife Maria Luisa of Parma, works that secured his election as a painter to the court.

The Madrid Period

Following the War of Independence, he was summoned to Madrid where, after he was elected first painter to the court in 1815, he worked during the reign of Ferdinand VII, the subsequent regency and even the beginning of the reign of Isabel.

Having chief responsibility of artistic affairs, he was in charge of controlling all the great projects carried out in the court of Ferdinand. His main artistic responsibilities were the creation and management of the Royal Painting Museum, support for the various artists attached to the court, and directing the decorating of royal sites. These made him the most sought-after painter in Madrid society.

He painted important portraits of the kings and queens (*Queen Maria Cristina de Borbon,* c. 1829; *Ferdinand VII with the uniform of the Order of the Toison de Oro,* 1831); members of Ferdinand's court, soldiers, important clergy; and ancient members of the aristocracy (*The Duke of San Carlos,* 1814). He also painted extraordinarily accurate and highly realistic portraits of officials of the court and of many other important personalities of the period, such as *Francisco de Goya* (1826).

62

FRANCISCO DE GOYA

Despite being trained in the Academic tradition, Francisco de Goya was soon able to distance himself from the Rococo and Neo-Classical currents that were favored in Spain during his lifetime. His painting technique allowed him to work using increasingly free forms and contexts, anticipating both Romantic and Impressionistic techniques. Dedicated to everyday subjects and to portraits, he was masterful in his denouncing not only the horrors of war but also of fraud and falseness.

Artistic Education and Early Years As a Painter

Francisco de Goya. The Parasol (1777). Oil on canvas, 59.75 × 41 in. The Prado, Madrid.

Francisco de Goya y Lucientes (1746–1828) was born in Fuendetodos (Zaragoza, Spain) and soon joined the studio of José Luzán, from whom he learned to draw by the traditional method of copying from engravings. At this time he began his relationship with the Bayeu family. In 1771 he traveled to Rome, where he painted Classical themes: *Sacrifice to Pan* and *Sacrifice to Vesta*.

On his return to Zaragoza, he received a commission to paint a fresco in one of the smaller domes of the Basilica of the Pillar, and later the mural cycle of the *Life of the Virgin* in the monastery of Aula Dei. Thanks to his master and brother-in-law Francisco Bayeu and to Mengs, in 1774 he started work as a cartoonist at the royal tapestry factory in Madrid. Between 1775 and 1792 he painted 63 works of popular themes, full of light and chromatic range, most of which were celebratory or light-hearted, such as *The Parasol*, *Blind Man's Buff* or *The Rag Doll*.

Engravings and Portraits

Goya began engraving in 1778, and his mastery in the technique culminated in the four series of engravings known as *Caprichos*, *Disasters*, *Tauromaquia*, and *Disparates*. In 1780 he joined the Academy of Fine Art in San Fernando, painting, as his first work there, the sober *Christ on the Cross*. For the last two decades of the century, he was actively engaged as a portraitist of members of high society (*The Count of Floridablanca*, *The Marquis of Pontejos*, *The Family of the Duke of Osuna*).

The New Pictorial Vision

Influenced by the revolutionary ideas of Europe, he acquired a growing political and social conscience. His portraits and compositions were inspired by life and superstition, culminating in the *Frescoes of Saint Anthony of Florida* in which he took a miracle by Saint Anthony as a pretext to show a multitude of everyday people. Witchcraft

THE ARTIST'S LIFE

1746 Born in Fuendetodos, Zaragoza.	Madrid, with similar lack of success.	**1799** Named first court painter.
1760 Joins the studio of José Luzán.	**1785** Is named deputy-director of the Royal Academy of Fine Art of San Fernando.	**1808** With the invasion of Napoleon's army begins the most intense period of his artistic career.
1763 Enters the competition of the Academy of San Fernando in Madrid, without success.	**1786** Along with Ramón Bayeu, is nominated painter to the king.	**1819** Acquires the Quinta del Sordo, to which he retires in deliberate isolation.
1766 Re-enters the competition of the Academy of San Fernando in	**1798** Paints the frescoes in the chapel of San Antonio de la Florida in Madrid.	**1828** Dies in Bordeaux.

Francisco de Goya. Charles IV and His Family (1800). Oil on canvas, 132.25 × 110.25 in. The Prado, Madrid.

and trickery were the main themes of the eight paintings he produced around 1798 for the Alameda of Osuna, among which were *Witches Sabbath* and *The Sabbat*. These were also themes he treated in his illustrations to fight against the ignorance and lack of education of the common people.

Final Period

Around 1812 to 1814 he painted various paintings in which he showed the cruelty of the Inquisition and represented popular traditions. Later he painted the fantastic themes that featured in his engravings and his *Black Paintings*, which

he painted in oil on the walls of his house, called Quinta del Sordo. When Fernando VII came to the throne, Goya lost royal favor and exiled himself in France, living in Bordeaux until his death in 1824.

Francisco de Goya. Court of the Inquisition *(1815–1819).*
Oil on board, 28.75 × 17 in. Museum of the Royal Academy of Fine Art of San Fernando, Madrid.

ROMANTICISM AND ACADEMIC GENRE

Before the arrival of Romanticism, the main themes of painters and sculptors were religion, mythology, and history, as well as portrait painting. As the new movement did not break dramatically with the pre-existing situation, artists incorporated the innovations of Romanticism without forsaking the importance that the Academy attached to these genres. Artistic dominance during this period came from the work both of Andalusian artists and from the great artists of the court.

The Academy of Fine Arts of Cadiz

At the end of the eighteenth century, Cadiz had become one of the most flourishing cities in Spain thanks to its commercial prosperity. The Cadiz Academy of Noble Arts was founded there in 1787. Juan Rodriguez Jiménez (1765–1830), who had trained in Cadiz and Seville, was the first painter whose work tended towards the Romantic. He was basically a painter of portraits and religious and historical themes, such as *The Marquis of La Romana Embarking His Troops in Denmark* (1808), although he is considered the initiator of genre painting with scenes from everyday life such as *The Dance of the Lantern*.

Other Artists

Joaquim Manuel Fernández (1781–1856) was also trained in Cadiz and Seville, as well as Madrid, and was the most important painter in this circle. Among his works, his private portraits, such as *Madam Maria Josefa de Corte de Gargollo* (c. 1832), are closest to the new Romantic spirit. A later artist from Cadiz was José Utreta (1827–1848), whose *Self-portrait* (1847) is one of the most suggestive in Spanish Romanticism. Among the artists who joined the Romantic movement

early on is the Cordoban artist Angel de Savedra y Ramírez de Baquedano, Duke of Rivas (1791–1865).

The Seville Academy of Fine Art

In the latter part of the nineteenth century, the city of Seville enjoyed an economic wealth and a cultural climate that greatly favored artistic activity which, along with the Romantic reputation of the city, produced an incomparable environment for the creation of new types and forms of art. Antonio Cabral Bejarano (1788–1861), a member of a famous dynasty, assumed leadership of the Seville School in 1850. As a painter, he produced various decorative and religious works in which his devotion to Murillo can be noted, as well as that to genre painting. He is most

David Roberts.
The Mosque at Cordoba.
The Prado, Casón del Buen Retiro, Madrid.

Joaquín Domínguez Bécquer. The Spanish Meet with the Moroccans to Negotiate a Peace Settlement *(1863). Oil on canvas, 231 × 124.75 in. The Prado, Casón del Buen Retiro, Madrid.*

famous, however, for his work as a portraitist (*The Marquis of Arco Hermoso and his Family*, 1833).

José Domínguez Bécquer (1805–1841), another painter from a similarly illustrious family, stands out mainly because of his contribution to the depiction of human characters and of sites in his genre painting. His cousin Joaquín played an important part in the artistic life of Seville, but it was his son Valeriano who became the most famous painter in the dynasty.

Religious Themes and Portraits

José Gutiérrez de la Vega (1791–1865) was, of all the Spanish painters of the nineteenth century, the one who best combined the tradition of Murillo with the Romantic spirit. His work also reflects the influence of British art.

Between 1845 and 1855 he produced his best work, with religious paintings such as *Saint Justa and Saint Rufina*

(c. 1846) and showed in some of his portraits a certain tendency toward popular customs and traditions with a Goyan flavor.

Another outstanding portrait painter was José María Romero (*The Children of the First Count of Ibarra*, 1852) who, along with Antonio María Esquivel, represented the pinnacle of Sevillian Romanticism.

Antonio María Esquivel. The Gathering of Poets *(1846). Oil on canvas, 84.25 × 56.75 in. The Prado, Madrid.*

FEDERICO DE MADRAZO

The two great court painters of the period were Federico de Madrazo and Carlos Luis de Ribera, who throughout their lives created the most notable synthesis between more moderate Romantic ideals and the continuation of the academic system. The latter system had a wide following in Spain through the main institutions of the state. The teaching, interest, and diffusion of their work extended beyond the limits of the court, and both artists represented a stylistic approach that spread beyond the second third of the nineteenth century.

The Man and His Training

Federico de Madrazo (1815–1894) was himself the son of an artist, José de Madrazo, from whom he received a careful artistic training. Federico de Madrazo was a painter whose life was an unstoppable succession of triumphs and public recognition. The most important decisions concerning artistic enterprises were referred to him; the important characters in the political and cultural life of the state posed for him; and with him began and was consolidated the so-called Purist branch of Spanish Romanticism. All this was possible thanks to the privileged personal situa-

tion that he enjoyed from a very young age which allowed him direct contact with the aristocrats and artists of the whole of Europe, as well as to an artistic training that was strengthened by frequent trips abroad, combined, of course, with his extraordinary talent and skill as a painter.

Federico de Madrazo.
Young Woman *(identity unknown).*
Romantic Museum, Madrid.

Emulating the decisions his father himself had made by staying first in Paris and later in Rome, Madrazo traveled to the French capital twice, the first time in 1833, attracted principally by the Purism of Ingres and by a desire to study the work of Gérard Gros, Delaroche, Vernet, and even Delacroix.

Time in Paris and Rome

During this period, up until his second visit to Paris, he painted a splendid series of portraits of the most important characters associated with the court in Madrid, such as his portraits of *The Marquise of Viluma, The Countess of Montijo* (both of 1836), and the beautiful, delicate portrait of *Luisa Garreta* (1837). His second stay in Paris was decisive in his artistic career. He was commissioned by King Louis

THE ARTIST'S LIFE

1815 Born in Rome.
1830 Admitted as Academician of Merit to the Royal Academy of Fine Art of San Fernando.
1833 Travels to Paris, where he meets Ingres and studies the work of the other French artists.
1835 In Madrid contributes to the Romantic magazine *The Artist* with a large number of graphic works.

1837–1839 Stays in Paris for the second time, enjoying the protection of Prosper Mérimée and Baron Taylor.
1840 Meets the Nazarenes in Rome.
1842 Returns to Madrid, where he works intensely as an artist, making numerous portraits.
1846 Becomes a member of the Academy of Fine Art of San Fernando.

1857 Elected first painter to the court.
1860 Becomes director of the Prado. Becomes a member of the judging panel for national exhibitions of Fine Art.
1866 Elected director of the Academy of Fine Art of San Fernando.
1894 Dies in Madrid.

Federico de Madrazo. Juan Contreras (1881). Oil on canvas. Army Museum, Madrid.

From the Nazarenes he learned the intellectual approach to art, similar to the techniques of the Purists, whose concepts he later abandoned in favor of a more chromatic approach closer to the tradition of Velázquez and Goya.

Amalia de Llano, aspires to win over the viewer with her intense gaze and pose. Another is the later portrait, *The Countess of Siruela* (1873), a painting with a diaphanous atmosphere and varied palette, which produces interesting shifts in color.

Among his male portraits stands out *Segismundo Moret* (1853), whose elegantly dressed figure silhouetted against a neutral background looks out with aristocratic arrogance. Also *The Count of Eleta* (1856), who is depicted looking falsely bohemian; or the private portraits, such as his daughter-in-law *Marià Fortuny* (1867), which shows a clear evolution, when it was made, toward Realism.

Philippe to paint a historical work, *Godofredo de Bouillon proclaimed King of Jerusalem* (1838), for the Crusade Gallery at the Palace of Versailles, which shows the privileged position he enjoyed, helped by the bourgeois king's Spanish affinities.

In Rome from 1840, he joined the followers of Friedrich Overbeck, a key figure with whom he shared a devotion for Italian painting and for Antonio van Dyck. At this time he completed a painting he had begun in Paris of *The Three Marys at the Sepulchre* (1842), one of the most significant and early works showing the Nazarene influence on Spanish painting.

Madrazo's Return to Madrid and a Career at Court

Following his return to Madrid, from 1842 he began an unstoppable career as a portraitist at the Spanish court. Of the many paintings he produced during this period for the royal family or for official institutions there are good portraits of Isabel II, although

there are also conventional paintings in which one can see all the details of his studio.

Splendid examples of his painting include his sweetly seductive portrait of *The Countess of Vilches* (1853), one of his best portraits, partly because of its use of color and partly because its subject, Doña

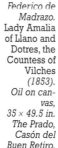

Federico de Madrazo. Lady Amalia of Llano and Dotres, the Countess of Vilches (1853). Oil on canvas, 35 × 49.5 in. The Prado, Casón del Buen Retiro, Madrid.

THE NAZARENE MOVEMENT AND THE CATALAN ARTISTS

At the height of the Romantic era, a large number of Catalan artists could be found in Rome. In accordance with one of the fundamental edicts of the Purist ideal, they were interested in the Medieval world, and through their dedication to this historical theme they tried to express a spirit of identity with the place where they had been born.

The Llotja Artists and the Nazarenes

There was very little direct contact between the main Spanish (Catalan) artists who arrived in Rome in the 1830s and the members of the Nazarenes, except for Friedrich Overbeck, who was the only member of the Nazarenes to live there until his death.

One of the first Romantics was Josep Arrau i Barba (1802–1872), who became interested in neo-Medievalism following a trip to Milan in 1831. Another artist of the same generation was Jaume Batlle Mir (1801–1865), an important engraver who had exhibitions in Madrid and

Barcelona that revealed his Romantic tendencies. Nazarene Purism was adopted by Pau Milà i Fontanals (1810–1883), but the three most important figures were Joaquim Espalter (1809–1880), Pelegrí Clavé (1811–1880), and Claudio Lorenzale (1815–1889), who spread their ideals following their return from Italy. The real importance of Milà i Fontanals lays more in his role as a theoretical forerunner and leader than in his artistic works.

The Work of Joaquim Espalter

Born in Sitges and trained at the Llotja School, Joaquim

Espalter soon moved to Marseille and Paris where, it seems, he met Gros. In 1833 he moved to Italy, where a few years later he successfully exhibited, in Florence, his works *Melancholy of a Young Heart* and *Dante and Virgil*, which were influenced by the Nazarene movement.

He returned to Spain in 1842 and settled in Madrid. There he painted several official works and made an important contribution to the artistic life of the city until his death. He was awarded numerous decorations and was elected a member of the Academy of San Fernando, as professor of drawing antiquity and apparel,

Claudio Lorenzale. The Death of Peter II the Great *(1870).*
Council Hall of the Town Hall of Vilafranca del Penedès, Barcelona.

Joaquim Espalter. Portrait of the Artist's Wife (1852). Oil on canvas, 35 × 44.5 in. Museum of Modern Art, Barcelona.

of painting at the Academy of Fine Art in Mexico, where he spent the most important stage of his career and where he played a key role in the organization of the artistic life of that country, while never setting aside painting.

Claudio Lorenzale

Born in Barcelona, though of Italian origin, Claudio Lorenzale studied at the Llotja and lived in Rome, on a scholarship, between 1837 and 1841, where he became a fervent follower of the doctrines of Friedrich Overbeck. Following his return to Barcelona in 1842, he traveled around Spain, and later worked as a professor at the Llotja, providing teaching that was to bear substantial fruit. He was dedicated to all genres, although he especially cultivated historical painting (*The Creation of the Barcelona Coat of Arms*, c. 1842–43) and portraits, and was one of Barcelona's most sought-after painters.

and from 1846 he was an official court painter.

Although he cultivated different genres, his religious paintings stand out, including several large-scale works. He also produced genre paintings, with Italian characters, as well as portraits, which are among his best works.

Pelegrí Clavé

Considered the most notable painter of the Catalan Purist group, Pelegrí Clavé was also a student at the Llotja. Awarded a scholarship in 1834 to go to Rome, there he produced Raphaelite paintings such as *The Good Samaritan* (1839). He was named director

Claudio Lorenzale. Queen Juana is Forbidden to Accompany the Prince of Viana to Barcelona (1870). Council Hall of the Town Hall of Vilafranca del Penedès, Barcelona.

COSTUMBRISTA AND LANDSCAPE PAINTING

The importance of *costumbrista* painting — painting of everyday life and customs — in Spain as a pictorial type was enormous. Proof of this is that, with the profusion of images relating to the Romantic myth of the country, *costumbrista* painting went beyond the limits of Romanticism itself as a cultural movement. At the same time, despite the fact that one cannot really talk of a school, but rather a series of individual artists who shared different views, it was with the diffusion of Romantic images that landscape painting reached its peak as an independent genre.

Manuel Cabral Bejarano. The Procession of Corpus.
Oil on canvas, 95.75 × 59.75 in. The Prado, Madrid.

Costumbrista Painting in Andalusia

The land of Andalusia provided the typical images that spread the Romantic myth of Spain. European travelers contributed to this phenomenon to a great extent, attracted to Andalusia more than to any other part of Spain. They encouraged the incorrect idea of identifying Andalusia with Spain, or, amounting to the same thing, thinking that Andalusian genre painting provided a true image of Spain. For this reason the main theme around which most of the genre painting revolved was the fiesta. Among the first *costumbrista* painters, José Elbo (1804–1844) was a sin-

gular figure in Andalusian Romanticism, while among the artists who were specifically dedicated to this genre, Manuel Cabral Bejarano (1827–1891) stands out as an artist of great imagination. So also do Joaquín Domínguez Bécquer (1817–1867), who was a highly skilled draftsman; Manuel Rodríguez de Guzmán (1818–1867), who imbued his paintings with a great deal of personality (*The Procession of Rocío*); and Valeriano Domínguez Bécquer (1833–1870), a painter whose career started in Seville, but who enriched his work with many other experiences, both in following the tradition of Goya and in his personal, direct contact with his surroundings.

Costumbrista Painting in Madrid

From a point of view of form as well as theme, the development of this genre painting in Madrid was intimately connected with the figure of Goya, whose importance was considerable. To this influence one must add the national schools that had traditionally developed genre painting, such as the Dutch School and above all the Flemish School, especially through the work of Teniers. Leonardo Alenza (1807–1845) was one of the key figures of the period, dedicating himself primarily to painting small, poignant, anecdotal paintings, as well as numerous portraits. Eugenio Lucas (1817–1870) was a virtuoso of painting whose multifaceted personality is reflected in the varied repertory of his pictorial subject matter (*The Laxative*), among which stands out his commitment to *costumbrista* painting.

Another interesting painter was Francisco Lameyer (1825–1877) who, attracted by the Oriental and exotic, visited Morocco at the same time as Marià Fortuny. Together with Jenaro Pérez Villaamil and Eugenio Lucas, he was one of the main painters of Oriental themes of the Romantic period.

The Leading Landscape Painters

Considered to be the most important Romantic Spanish landscape painter, Jenaro Pérez Villaamil was born in El Ferrol and moved to Madrid while still young. In 1823 he had to interrupt his studies there and join the army following the invasion of the French (the "Hundred Thousand Sons of St. Louis"). Quartered in Cadiz until 1830, it was there that his life changed, and from then on he devoted himself to painting.

In 1833 he traveled in Andalusia and met David Roberts (1796–1854) in Seville, forming a friendship that was to be decisive in his definitive artistic direction. He joined the court around 1834, and his various trips around Spain provided him with themes for his paintings, which he made the most of in works like *Seville in the Time of the Arabs* (1848).

Among the Andalusian landscape artists, noteworthy were Manuel Barrón (1814–1884) and Andrés Cortés (c.1815–c.1879), and among the Catalans, Fransesc Xavier Parcerisa (1803–1876) and Lluís Rigalt (1814–1894).

Leonardo Alenza. Romantic Suicide. *Romantic Museum, Madrid.*

Eugenio Lucas. The Laxative. *Oil on canvas, 151.5 × 191 in. The Prado, Cásón del Buen Retiro, Madrid.*

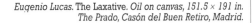

THE PRE-RAPHAELITES

The Pre-Raphaelites were exponents of an artistic movement that started in Great Britain in the middle of the nineteenth century. They reacted against the academic precepts of official culture, Victorian conventionality, and the negative aspects of industrial society in order to bring modern art to the country. For this reason they tried to restore a more spontaneous art inspired by nature, reflected in the work of painters of the past dating to Raphael, from whom the group derived their name. With time, the Pre-Raphaelite artists had an influence on many aspects of their environment.

The Seed of the New Movement

The Pre-Raphaelite Brotherhood was formed in London in 1848 with the aim of endowing artistic works with a significance that was capable of transmitting a message, as had been the case with Christian painting.

From this point of view, subjects such as landscapes or portraits were given secondary importance in favor of social themes inspired by the legends and literature of the Middle Ages, the Bible, Shakespeare, and especially contemporary writers.

Within the social context in which the group was formed, one must not forget that in 1850 the Royal Academy, an institution of great prestige, began to lose its monopoly as a consequence of the new schools of drawing created by William Dyce. Furthermore, the particular idiosyncrasy of the British meant that when they chose and depicted contemporary themes, the Pre-Raphaelites were also to some extent educating their potential public.

The Creators of the *Pre-Raphaelite Brotherhood*

The homogeneity of the group's artistic life barely lasted four years, although this was enough time to develop a characteristic style of painting that was reflected by the Brotherhood's members and their followers. The founders were William Holman Hunt (1827–1910), John Everett Millais (1829–1896), and Dante Gabriel Rossetti (1828–1882).

Later, the founders admitted into their group the painter James Collinson, the sculptor Thomas Woolner, the art critic Frederic George Stephens, and William Michael, the brother of Rossetti, as a chronicler.

Walter Dewell later joined the group, which also was a hub for other painters, including William Dyce, Arthur Hughes, Frederick Arthur Sandys, and others.

Ford Madox Brown (1821–1893) also was a supporter of the London movement, although he was never a full member of it.

William Dyce. Pegwell Bay in Kent. A recollection of October 5th 1858 *(1860).* The National Gallery, London.

David Wilkie. The Scottish Touch. *The Wallace Collection, London.*

The Pre-Raphaelites As an Inspiration for Other Movements

The Pre-Raphaelites were defended with authority by John Ruskin (1819–1900), the most influential critic in Great Britain during the nineteenth century, who was also an artist and naturalist. Before they disbanded, the Brotherhood received other new members such as Edward Coley Burne-Jones (1833–1898) and William Morris (1834–1896), who both further developed Morris's principles of renovation.

The Pre-Raphaelites had a great influence on art at the end of the nineteenth century, from Modernism to Symbolism, thanks to the work of Morris himself, Walter Crane (1845– 1915), and Aubrey Beardsley (1872–1898), who took the Pre-Raphaelite movement as his starting point.

Accepting the Pre-Raphaelites

Initially, the Pre-Raphaelites were met by public and critical hostility, although they went on to become important as a modern artistic group. They spoke out, defended themselves, and gained publicity through their own magazine *The Germ*.

It wasn't long before the group began to make itself heard and to enjoy the sympathy of supporters and collectors who accepted that, just as had happened with Classicism and in the same way as the Nazarenes were inspired by the Middle Ages, this new generation of artists would turn their attention to the past to regenerate themselves from purer sources from the period of the Primitives.

Edward Coley Burne-Jones.
The Merciful Knight.
Oil on canvas, 27.25 × 39.5 in.
Museum and Art
Gallery, Birmingham.

DANTE GABRIEL ROSSETTI

Dante Gabriel Rossetti was an artist whose work is rooted in sensuality and anti-naturalism. The ideas of the Pre-Raphaelites and his own individualism caused him a great deal of conflict. Also esteemed as a highly cultured poet, on account of his youth and creative strength, he became the soul of the group and of its magazine, *The Germ*, a publication that he defended in artistic and religious arguments. Thus, despite the fact that his painting is a faithful reflection of a supremely personal philosophy, this did not prevent it from influencing artists of the caliber of William Morris.

The Soul of the Pre-Raphaelite Brotherhood

A British painter and poet, Dante Gabriel Rossetti was the son of an Italian patriot and poet from Abruzzo, exiled in London. His mother's brother, John Polidori, had been the secretary to Lord Byron. His sister Cristina was an important lyric poet in the Victorian age. He stood out in this stimulating circle thanks to his surprising precocity, translating Dante's *Vita Nuova* and poetry by Guido Cavalcanti into English.

At the age of fourteen he had already decided to dedicate his life to art, despite his disgust at the official line of the Sass drawing school and the Royal Academy. During his years as a student, he produced sketches in Chinese ink based on the style and subjects of the English caricaturists. From 1846 on, he dedicated himself to literary illustration: for example Meinhold's *The Witch of Ambar*,

Dante Gabriel Rossetti. The Girlhood of the Virgin Mary (1849). Oil on canvas, 25.5 × 32.25 in. The Tate Gallery, London.

Dante Gabriel Rossetti. Proserpine (1877). Oil on canvas, 23.25 × 45 in. The Tate Gallery, London.

Chamisso's *Peter Schemihl*, and Poe's *The Raven*.

Rossetti's Work

On his return to London following a trip to Paris in 1849, he dedicated a large part of his time to the publication of *The Germ*, with poetry, critical texts, and works by members of the Brotherhood. In two of his youthful works, *The Girlhood of the Virgin Mary* (1849) and *Ecce ancilla Domini!* (1850), one can appreciate, in addition to the influence of the Nazarenes, the typically Pre-Raphaelite desire to reinterpret the artistic vision

Dante Gabriel Rossetti. Dante's Dream at the Time of the Death of Beatrice *(1871).*
Oil on canvas, 124 × 82 in. Walker Art Gallery, Liverpool.

of the fifteenth century, and above all what is understood as the "mystical innocence" of painters like Fra Angelico.

The Artist's Influence

Rossetti's painting lacks the analytical realism of the other members of the group, partly because he preferred free, immediate media such as pastel, watercolor, or drawing. Even so, he was the most influential artist in the movement, particularly on account of his poetic work, of which his painting was often a direct reflection.

In his work, the representation of the female figure, of the "donna angelicata" (*Beata Beatrix*, 1863; *Dante's Dream at* the Time of the Death of Beatrice, 1871) or of perverse creatures (*Astarte Syriaca*, 1877) is at its most significant, and is where the ambiguity of all his art is best exemplified: the aspiration to an ideal world, to a legendary past, and a mixture of sensuality and disquiet.

THE ARTIST'S LIFE

1828 Born in London.
1846 Produces a series of literary illustrations, of which the ones dedicated to Goethe and Poe show his rapid evolution.
1848 His drawing *Margaret in Church* shows his new stylistic direction, which is similar to the later direction of the Pre-Raphaelites. He studies in the studios of Ford Madox Brown and of William Holman Hunt, and forges an artistic alliance with them. Along with other artists, he founds the Pre-Raphaelite Brotherhood in London.
1849 For the first time, the members of the group decide to send their work to the summer exhibitions. He moves to Paris and Bruges together with William Holman Hunt.
1850 Begins publishing the magazine *The Germ.*
1854 Begins his composition *Found*, a painting inspired by the reports published three years previously by Henry Mayhew about the working class and prostitutes.
1855–1860 Finds his true artistic style, centered on watercolor and drawing.
1882 Dies in Birchington-on-Sea.

JOHN EVERETT MILLAIS

The emotional drive is less intense in the work of John Everett Millais than in the other Pre-Raphaelites. His painting frequently reflects the anecdotal and the everyday, coming close to continental naturalist painting, with which he also shared a certain tendency toward the pathetic and sentimental. Without discounting his artistic interpretation and reflection, in his later paintings the balance seems to dissolve in favor of a more academic style.

Millais' Contribution

Among the Pre-Raphaelites, John Everett Millais was the supreme painter. He was a man of great culture devoid of all gratuitous personal exhibitionism who converted the spiritual stimulus of the Pre-Raphaelites into a reason for attaining higher goals rather than following the easy but well-remunerated path of the Victorian society painter.

Along with Dante Gabriel Rossetti, he became the most widely ranging artist in the Brotherhood, to which he added his confident technique, his ambition, and his indisputable vision, thus contributing notoriously to the success of the Brotherhood and to its being understood in terms of its ideological as well as pictorial contributions.

John Everett Millais. The Blind Girl (1856). Birmingham Museum, Great Britain.

John Everett Millais. Ophelia (1852). Oil on canvas, 44 × 30. The Tate Gallery, London.

The Role of the Critics

After the initials PRB became known as identifying members of the Pre-Raphaelite Brotherhood and they revealed their objectives in *The Germ*, the group used the Universal Exhibition of 1851 to prepare an attack on conservatism. The Brotherhood's works were accused by the critics of being abrupt and awkward, and the work of Millais of being pictorially blasphemous. At the show, he exhibited a work entitled *The Woodman's Daughter* based on a poem by Coventry Patmore, written between 1839–1841, in which he threw Victorian sentimentalism into relief. His other two contributions to the exhibition represented an evolution toward a more fluid style: *Mariana*, the heroine of a poem by Alfred Tennyson, published in 1830, and *The Return of the Dove to the Ark*, a much more intimate work.

The Consolidation of His Prestige

Meanwhile, Millais continued to win recognition and prestige, supported by figures as important as John Ruskin, who even wrote in the *Times* arguing in favor of the Pre-Raphaelites. Together with William Holman Hunt, Millais moved to the country and in Cuddington painted the opulent background of his work *Ophelia*,

John Everett Millais. Autumn Leaves (1856). City Art Gallery, Manchester.

which was a delightful observation of nature, although it is also a surprisingly fascinating painting and one that is thematically revolutionary on account of its representation of the drowned young woman. Melancholy characterized one of the last stages of his life, as can be seen in works like *The Blind Girl* and *Autumn Leaves*, both from 1856. Later, genre painting rounded off his artistic career, and he became the most highly sought-after chronicler of society of the period.

THE ARTIST'S LIFE

1829 Born in Southampton.
1838 Attends Henry Sass's art school. Wins a silver medal from the Society of Arts.
1846 Receives the gold medal for a biblical painting in oil, painted according to the purist academic tradition. Meets William Holman Hunt, whose friendship helps his artistic work mature.
1851 Exhibits various works at the Universal Exhibition.
1851–1852 Moves to the country in order to paint the background of his famous painting *Ophelia*.
1853 Paints the portrait of Ruskin at Glenfinlas in Scotland, where they spend their holidays together.
1855 Paints the work *The Rescue*, about abandoned children, a highly appreciated theme in Victorian painting.
1896 Elected director of the Royal Academy. Dies in London.

EDWARD COLEY BURNE-JONES

A follower of the teaching of Dante Gabriel Rossetti, Burne-Jones developed his own style
to a point of refinement and idealization. His angelic female figures are the result of the
direct influence of his master, pure with the slightly perturbing sensuality of their models.
Their ambiguous strokes and sense of disquiet situates Burne-Jones's work between
the Pre-Raphaelites and the Symbolist art of the end of the nineteenth century,
and thus they represent an extension in the ideas of the group's original ideas.

The Continuation of an Idea

*Edward Coley
Burne-Jones.
Sidonia von
Borke (1860).
The Tate Gallery,
London.*

It was toward 1853, a time
when the Pre-Raphaelites were
beginning to make their works
and their objectives more
widely known, that the members of the group began to
follow individual paths. Nevertheless, thanks to Burne-Jones
and William Morris, some time
after the foundation of the
group, they managed to join
into a second alliance that was
somewhat different in format
from the first one, but pre-
served its objectives.

That year, both men entered
Exeter College, Oxford, where
they became interested in the
Middle Ages, read John Ruskin,
and focused their attention on
the work of the Pre-Raphaelites.
Their readings helped their
decision to abandon ecclesiastic careers to become artists.
A major factor in this decision
was their reading of the prose
work by Sir Thomas Malory, *La
Morte d'Arthur.*

Edward Coley Burne-Jones. The Hours. *Sheffield Art Gallery, Great Britain.*

Avoiding Reality

Burne-Jones was an artist who had never identified with the century. Extremely sensitive, for him religion was a point of escape, and when he began his ecclesiastic career he did so thinking, above all, of a retired, monastic life, something he was not to achieve until much later. Another escape point was drawing caricatures, where he showed his great skill with pen and ink. He rejected the naturalist tendencies of other artists such as William Holman Hunt.

In 1855 he traveled with Morris to France to visit its cathedrals, the Musée Cluny, and the Louvre. On their return they founded *The Oxford and Cambridge Magazine*, a periodical envisioned and funded by Morris that followed similar lines as its predecessor, *The Germ*.

Burne-Jones' Pictorial Work

The thematic tendencies of this Pre-Raphaelite artist show that he found refuge in religious topics (*The Adoration of the Magi and the Shepherds*,

Edward Coley Burne-Jones. The Beguiling of Merlin (1874). The Lady Lever Art Gallery, Port Sunlight, Cheshire.

1861–1862), classical mythology (*The Story of Pygmalion* 1869–1879), and Medieval legends (*King Copetua and the Beggar Maid*, 1884). He created a major body of decorative work, which he produced on Morris's printing press, and designed more than a hundred designs for stained glass, mosaics for the apse of the American church in Rome, carpets, tiles, ceramics, and furniture decorations. His paintings of what is called the Perseus cycle, which decorate the reception room of the old London house of the British politician Arthur James Balfour (1875), reflect the world of Burne-Jones extremely well, and it is here that this artist's form of painting finds its most perfect expression.

THE ARTIST'S LIFE

1833 Born in Birmingham.
1853 Attends Exeter College, Oxford.
1855 Travels with Morris to France to admire its cathedrals. Cooperates in the founding of *The Oxford and Cambridge Magazine*.
1857 Participates in the decoration of the Oxford Union. Begins his designs for stained-glass windows at Bradford College, Oxford.
1858 Creates his first sketch for Oxford Cathedral, with the legend of the local Saint Frideswide.
1859 Travels to Italy to study the art period immediately before and after Raphael.
1862 Travels to Italy for a second time.
1877 Has his first exhibition at the Groswenor Gallery.
1898 Dies in Fulham, London.

WILLIAM MORRIS AND THE "ARTS AND CRAFTS" MOVEMENT

As a movement for reform of applied arts, the Arts and Crafts movement was started in Great Britain toward the middle of the nineteenth century in an attempt to halt the increasing deterioration in aesthetic quality of common, everyday objects brought about by industrial production, something that was evident by the Universal Exhibition in London in 1851. On a theoretical level, the influence of John Ruskin was fundamental in its advocacy for a return to Medieval artistic production values.

The Beginning of an Idea

In 1754, with the foundation of the Society of Arts, the British government stimulated the cooperation between Arts and Crafts. Reformed by Prince Albert in 1847 Ruskin and the other members of the Pre-Raphaelite Brotherhood had, some years beforehand, given classes in public design schools and instilled in their students—future goldsmiths, jewelers, cabinet-makers, lithographers, draftsmen, and so on—their ideas on appreciation of nature and on the creative potential of art.

At the beginning of the nineteenth century, prefabrication and mass production had decimated the trade guilds, along with the traditional crafts. The idea of combining art and industry was put forward in order to offer work to the craftsmen and to raise the aesthetic quality of fabricated products. Thus, as art and industry became increasingly more compatible, there was an increasing move to recreate the Medieval tradition of the craftsmen. For an artist like Ruskin, Medieval craftwork expressed happiness, while William Morris also shared enthusiasm over its recovery.

William Morris and "Arts and Crafts"

This resurgence in traditional crafts came to be known as the "Arts and Crafts" movement. The movement took its name from the "Arts and Crafts Exhibition Society," founded in London in 1888. One of the main protagonists of this movement was Morris himself, who was radically opposed to the industrialization of design and insisted that art should be created by man for man's sake. Despite wanting to gain widespread acceptance for his ideas, he could not offer a solution to the economic problem that objects manufactured by hand were more expensive and, therefore, only within reach of the wealthiest members of society. Nevertheless, his ideas were considered, so that during the twentieth century artists began to create objects for industrial mass production and, in this way, introduced design to the general public.

Figurative Models

The company created by Morris in 1861, called Morris, Marshall, Faulkner and Co., created all types of objects for indoor, everyday use, including wallpaper, colored glass, carpets, fabrics, upholstery, furniture, and so on, along the lines of Medieval workshops. Artists such as Morris himself,

William Morris.
La Belle Iseult
(1858). Oil
on canvas,
19.75 ×
28.25 in.
The Tate
Gallery,
London.

Morris & Company. Painted handicraft (detail) from the residence of the Duke of Carlisle, Green Palace, London (c.1880). 472.5 × 39.25 in. (in total). Musée d'Orsay, Paris.

Dante Gabriel Rossetti, Walter Crane, Ford Madox Brown, and Edward Coley Burne-Jones worked for the company. Their designs achieved widespread popularity, while at the same time introduced styles that conditioned the public taste.

They favored drawings combining flowers and birds in the intertwined style of Celtic reliefs, Medieval illuminated manuscripts, and tapestry designs. For these they found inspiration in the *Grammar of Ornament* (1856), the work of the architect and designer Owen Jones, which was a rich source of designs originating in many cultures and of multiple techniques, from tapestry to mosaic.

William Morris. Woman Playing the Harp (1872–1874). Glass panel. Victoria and Albert Museum, London.

The Renovation and Subsequent Evolution of Typography

Using the same figurative models, Morris also renovated the art of typography with the foundation in 1890 of the Kelmscott Press at Merton Abbey.

His refined, handmade editions, such as the *Complete Works of Geoffrey Chaucer* spread a taste for books in Gothic typeface, illustrated with engravings, and characterized by extremely rich, thematic ornamentation. In this way, the whole "Arts and Crafts" movement generated numerous initiatives, such as the Art Workers' Guild of Crane and others in 1882, and Arthur Mackmurdo's Century Guild and Charles Robert Ashbee's Guild and School of Handicraft in 1888.

In this same year, the above mentioned Arts and Crafts Exhibition Society was formed, holding exhibitions every four years in London until 1912. The exhibitions, featured furniture, upholstery, artifacts, fabrics, and so on, with the participation of artists like Morris, Ashbee, Crane, Charles Francis Annesley Voysey, William Richard Lethaby, and many others.

FRENCH REALISM

Emerging in the middle of the nineteenth century, Realism succeeded Romanticism as a reaction against the correct style of the salons and against the subjective, fantastic visions of the Romantics. However, the Realists did not rely on the Romantics' great innovations in techniques when it came to painting. For the Realists, reality inspired the arts, and they set aside any preconceived ideas of beauty. At the same time, the artist kept subjective interpretation out of his or her work. Lifelike daily scenes now substituted for earlier themes.

The Barbizon School

The Realists expressed new concepts that aroused controversy in a society that was split between opposing and supporting them. Realism was a movement that summarized the feelings and convictions that were held by a large group of promising young artists and that formed the base of what would be the first major artistic movement of the modern era, namely Impressionism.

The foundations of the Realist representation of landscape can be found in what is called the Barbizon School, also known as the School of Fontainebleau or the landscape school of 1830, whose name came from the location — a village close to Fontainebleau — to which Théodore Rousseau moved in 1835.

Virgile Narcisse Díaz de la Peña.
The Jean de Paris Heights in the Forest of Fontainebleau (1867).
Oil on canvas, 41.75 × 34 in.
Musée d'Orsay, Paris.

It was he who, with the help of Camille Corot, led a group of artists such as Jean François Millet, Jules Dupré, Constant Troyon, Charles Daubigny, Antoine Louis Barye, Alexandre Gabriel Décamps, Virgile Narcisse Díaz de la Peña, and others. As a meeting point with nature, it was a place for cultural exchanges and long, creative retreats that helped

these artists further their study of atmospheric changes and light effects.

Camille Corot

Camille Corot (1796–1875) was born into a wealthy family of merchants. He trained with Michallon and later with Bertin, both landscape artists

Théodore Rousseau. Forest in Winter at Sunset (1845–1846). Oil on canvas, 102.25 × 64 in. Metropolitan Museum of Art, New York.

Jean Baptiste Camille Corot. Morning. Dance of the Nymphs (1850). Oil on canvas, 51.5 × 38.5 in. Musée d'Orsay, Paris.

with Classical tastes. His first stay in Italy (1825–1828) allowed him to create a very original style of painting, characterized by its vision of light (*The Coliseum seen from the Farnese Gardens*, 1826; *The Town of Castello Sant'Elia near Nepi*, 1826–1827). In 1834 he returned to Italy after spending a few years residing in Paris, the forest of Fontainebleau, and various places in the provinces.

Success was not slow in shining on him. Nevertheless, he distanced himself from fame and continued his pictorial investigation, becoming one of the first painters to work a *plein air* (in the open air) in order to transfer nature onto the canvas in a spontaneous maneuver. The freshness of his palette and his search for tonal and light values made him a forerunner of the Impressionists.

Honoré Daumier and Lithography

Honoré Daumier (1808–1879), the son of a glass-blower, moved to Paris from his hometown of Marseille in 1816. He trained as an apprentice painter with Alexandre Lenoir, a little-known artist who passed on to his pupil

his admiration for Titian and Rubens, and then later attended the Académie Suisse. He initially dedicated himself to lithography, in which he achieved great prestige thanks to his work in *La Caricature*, a periodical hostile to the French government of Louis Philippe. Some of his work cost him a series of prison sentences.

Daumier's Dedication to Painting

A friend of Corot, Rousseau, and Millet, Daumier focused on painting from 1860 onward. His work *The First Swim* (1860) can

perhaps be compared with the work of Millet, whose influence is also evident in the work *The Washerwoman* (1860–1862). A few years earlier (1857–1860) he painted *The Stamp Collector*, a work that showed his great ability at depicting the velvet blacks of lithography and dark colors. His last paintings grow ever closer to the style of Jean Honoré Fragonard in their fine, light brushwork, a technique that can be seen in *The Painter's Studio* (1869).

Honoré Daumier. The Third Class Carriage (1863–1865). Oil on canvas, 35.5 × 25.75. Metropolitan Museum of Art, New York.

JEAN FRANÇOIS MILLET

Jean François Millet has an unarguable place in history as an artist who opened up a new path in painting through the representation of the lives of farm workers. These paintings, in which he dealt with country themes in a style similar to the Dutch Realist tradition, are artistic reproductions of real life that convey a special vision of peasant society. A focused interest in depicting a dignified image of the lives of these people and their work is evident in all of them.

Realism in Jean François Millet

The origin of this type of art, rooted in an agenda that had never previously been advanced with such clarity, can be found in Millet's own childhood and adolescence. Millet (1814–1875) was the son of well-to-do farm workers in Contentín, and was born in the small village of Gruchy, near Gréville (France). At the age of twenty, he left the rural environment to devote himself to painting, receiving his early teaching in Cherbourg at the hands of Charles Langlois. He moved to Paris in 1838 where, thanks to a scholarship, he became a pupil of Paul Delaroche, studied at the Atelier Suisse and viewed the masterpieces of the Louvre. In 1847 he struck up a friendship with Honoré Daumier, Jules Dupré, Constant Troyon, and the critic Sensier.

Jean François Millet. Spring at Barbizon *(1868–1873). 43.75 × 33.75 in. Musée d'Orsay, Paris.*

At the Salon of 1848 he exhibited his first painting on a peasant theme, *The Winnower*. In the same year he moved to Barbizon, where he spent the rest of his life, apart from a few short trips to Cherbourg (1854 and 1870) and Vichy (1866 and 1868).

The Origin of His Rural Subject Matter

Millet was not the first artist to deal with rural-based themes in a dignified manner. During the sixteenth and seventeenth centuries, many Dutch painters, particularly Bruegel, faithfully represented the true nature of peasants and their lives. In common with the Barbizon group, Millet was searching for realism as a precise reflection of an ideological choice, which was, essentially, an escape from

Jean François Millet. The Woodcutter. 11.5 × 15 in. The Louvre, Paris.

the inhuman conditions of life in the city. An important element in the consolidation of Realism in the nineteenth century, apart from the influence exerted on it by Gustave Courbet, was the praise of the worker, the new hero born out of the uprisings of 1848 which, in Millet, coincided with a deep and anti-rhetorical understanding of peasant life. Thus many of his paintings of popular subjects are examples of a common theme, scenes of laborers hard at work sowing or reaping, of animals and peasants, involved in everyday activities and, very occasionally, resting after the day's work.

Millet's Skill

Millet's representational simplicity and, particularly, the compassion that is implicit in his paintings, had a deep impression on the public and on many painters for several decades, including Josef Israëls (1824–1911), Giovanni Segantini (1858–1899) and, above all, Vincent van Gogh (1853–1890). Despite the fact that his paintings do not show any greater relationship with color than, for example, the Nazarenes, and like them tended toward the symbolic, it was the peculiar monumentality that can be seen in his figures that gave his art its unique aesthetic.

Jean François Millet. The Evening Prayer *(1858–1859). Oil on canvas, 26 × 21.75 in. Musée d'Orsay, Paris.*

Jean François Millet. The Gleaners *(1857). Oil on canvas, 43.75 × 33.75 in. Musée d'Orsay, Paris.*

THE ARTIST'S LIFE

1814 Born in Gruchy, near Gréville (France).

1834 Receives his first artistic training in Cherbourg.

1838 Moves to Paris, where he studies with Paul Delaroche and at the Atelier Suisse.

1838–1848 Lives in Paris.

1847 Comes into contact with some of the artists of the Barbizon School.

1848 Exhibits his work *The Winnower* at the Salon, his first work on a rural theme. Moves to Barbizon, a place that signifies a return to nature and to the rural environment.

1850–1860 Dedicates himself primarily to painting the works of rural life that will make him famous worldwide.

1863 Begins painting occasional landscape works for the first time.

1875 Dies in Barbizon.

GUSTAVE COURBET

Gustave Courbet, the indisputable master of Realism, was one of those artists who are convinced that artists should only paint what they can perceive with their own senses, meaning the people, places, and things that surrounded them. As a result, he opposed mythological, historical, or literary themes that were so fashionable during this period. He stands out for his pictorial technique, which was very different from that of his Naturalist contemporaries who represented detail meticulously.

The Training of a Master from the Provinces

Gustave Courbet (1819–1877) was born into a family of well-off landowners in Ornans, a small French town near the border of Switzerland. After a period of training in Besançon as an apprentice to Jacques-Louis David, he moved to Paris in 1840 to dedicate himself to painting full-time, and there attended the Atelier Suisse. The central foundation of his pictorial training was the careful observation of the masterpieces of Flemish, Venetian, and Dutch painting of the sixteenth and seventeenth centuries that he was able to copy in the Louvre.

Courbet learned his painting technique principally from Veláz-quez and Zurbarán, his manipulation of paint and the depiction of light and shade from Rembrandt and Franz Hals, and his composition and the representation of space from David.

The Consolidation of Realism

Courbet achieved his mastery of Realist themes during the period from 1848 to 1857. His new vision is reflected in works like *Dusk at Orense* and *Peasants at Flagey Returning from the Fair*, paintings in which he depicted both the peasants and bourgeois members of rural society with such minute detail that he changed what up until then had been considered scenes from genre painting into historical painting. His work *Village Maidens* (1851) showed the passion he felt for the materiality of nature, and he anticipated in his background landscapes the focus that Cézanne would give to this type of subject matter at the end of the nineteenth century. In 1853 he exhibited *The Bathers*, a painting that caused a great scandal among society of the period.

Gustave Courbet. Village Maidens *(1851).*
Oil on canvas, 102.75 × 76.75 in. Metropolitan Museum of Art, New York.

Gustave Courbet. Burial at Ornans (1849–1850). Oil on canvas, 262 × 124 in. Musée d'Orsay, Paris.

Later Works

In 1855, the year of the International Exhibition, the jury accepted a series of his works, but rejected two that in the eyes of the painter were among the most important: *Burial at Ornans* and *The Painter's Studio*.

In 1875, his work *Young Ladies on the Banks of the Seine (Summer)* was also the cause of a scandal because of its uncustomary depiction of two women in a moment of fatigue, although the atmosphere depic-

ted in the painting anticipates the world of Impressionistic investigation. His later style evolved with the depiction of

figures with characteristic, clean outlines, a far cry from any Romantic or Academic influence (*The Studio*, 1855).

Gustave Courbet. Young Ladies on the Banks of the Seine (1875). Oil on canvas, 82 × 69 in Musée du Petit Palais, Paris.

THE ARTIST'S LIFE

1819   Born in Ornans (France).
1840   Moves to Paris to devote himself to painting.
1844   Participates in the Salon for the first time, with the painting *Self-Portrait* or *Courbet with Black Dog*.
1847   Travels to Holland, a country where the work of Rembrandt influences him deeply.

1848–1857 Consolidates the Realist element of his painting, with works like *Peasants at Flagey Returning from the Fair*.
1849   Wins a medal for his work *Dusk at Ornans*.
1860   Paints numerous female nudes as an unusual way of getting close to reality.
1870   Participates in the activities of the Paris Commune.

1873   After escaping from prison, flees to Switzerland.
1874   Is tried again and given a heavy fine for being found guilty of demolishing the Vendôme column.
1875   His painting *Young Ladies on the Banks of the Seine (Summer)* causes a great scandal.
1877   Dies at Vevey.

GERMAN NATURALISM

In Germany, the artistic movement equivalent to French Realism was called Naturalism. Despite the fact that its objectives are comparable to those of the Realists, neither the art of Honoré Daumier nor Gustave Courbet can be called Naturalist; however, the term can be applied to the works of Adolph Menzel. The different attitudes of these three painters toward nature reflects the differences that existed between nineteenth century painting in France and Germany.

German Naturalism and the Figure of Adolph Menzel

Although there are similarities in their aesthetic beliefs, the contrast between French Realism and German Naturalism implies more precise and determined disparities.

There was no contemporary parallel in France with the extreme Naturalism that occurred in Germany, a fact that can be explained by the tendency toward excess that German art had always shown. Adolph Menzel was considered the consummate Naturalist painter, displaying in his work, with extraordinary clarity, all the Naturalist tendencies.

Born in 1815, Menzel began his artistic career as an illustrator under the tutelage of his father, who had founded a lithography workshop in Berlin. Following the death of his father, Menzel was obliged to support the family and began to make use of all the training he had received as a printer.

The World of Illustration and Paintings

Menzel's first works of importance were the 400 illustrations he did for Frank Kugler's *Geschicte Friedrichs des Grossen*, published between 1840 and 1842. These were followed by other, similar works, full of allusions and symbolism. Like the other Naturalists interested in history, Menzel used them to make studies of the period that included people and objects, an approach he incorporated in his later historical paintings.

He quickly became famous for his singular early Impressionist style, and, during the period following this stage in his career, he painted a series of landscapes and interiors that did not become famous until after his death, but from then on they were considered among

Adolph Menzel. Frederick the Great's Flute Concerto in Sanssouci. *Staatliche Museen, Berlin.*

Jean-Louis-Ernest Meissonier. Napoleon on Campaign in 1814 *(1864).*
Oil on canvas, 44 × 20 in. Musée d'Orsay, Paris.

the most brilliant pictorial works of the nineteenth century. These paintings, such as *Garden of Prince Albert's Palace in Berlin* (1846), *The Potsdam-Berlin Railway,* and *The Artist's Sister with a Candle,* both from 1847, can be considered to be works of early Impressionism and were inspired by the works of Blechen, Dahl, and Constable.

The Followers of Adolph Menzel's Work

Among the painters who were impressed by Menzel's work was Jean-Louis-Ernest Meissonier (1815–1891), who in turn was greatly esteemed by Menzel. His paintings of soldiers, as well as the paintings of soldiers and of society painted by Anton von Werner (1843–1915), show that exaggerated Naturalism in historical paintings can lead to genre painting and to an unreal way of representing it. Specialists of other types of painting, such as the watercolor artist Carl Werner (1808–1904), found themselves morally obliged to admire the

richness of Menzel's art. Menzel's true followers were not just these artists, but everyone who could understand his genius as a painter and draftsman. These artists included Max Lieber mann and Max Slevoght. Outside Germany, he was also admired by Edgar Degas. The French

artist was the only one of his contemporaries of comparable excellence, not just in drawing and his rendering of graphic and pictorial effects, but also in his conception of the human figure.

Edgar Degas. Portrait of James Tissot *(1866–1868). Oil on canvas, 44 × 59.5 in. Musée d'Orsay, Paris.*

WILHELM LEIBL AND HIS CIRCLE OF ARTISTS

Influenced by Gustave Courbet's Realism, Wilhelm Leibl interpreted the work of the French master in the vein of the late Romantic tradition, painting poignant scenes from daily and rural life that were characterized by a high degree of fidelity in their interpretation. His portrait work, which was more similar in some respects to Impressionism, was critically acclaimed. The painters in his group tried to duplicate the tonal coherence of his works.

The Work of Wilhelm Leibl

Wilhelm Leibl (1844–1900) was born in Cologne (Germany) and studied at the Munich Academy under the tutorship of the painter of historical themes Karl Theodor von Piloty (1826–1865) and the genre painter Arthur Ramberg (1819–1875). It was during his artistic maturity that Leibel met Courbet, whose influence is obvious in works like *The Critics* (1868) and in the *Portrait of Madame Gedon*, painted in the same year and exhibited at the Universal Exhibition in Munich in 1869. Courbet, who also exhibited that year, showed his

Wilhelm Leibl. The Spinner *(1892). Staatliche Museen, Berlin.*

*Wilhelm Leibl.
Mina Gedon
(1868).
37.75 × 47 in.
Neue
Pinakothek,
Munich.*

approval of Leibl's work and suggested he should move to Paris, where he again exhibited and won a prize for the *Portrait of Madame Gedon*. Leibl stayed in the French capital until 1870, the year in which the Franco-Prussian War broke out, painting two of his most famous works, *Old Parisian Woman* (1870) and *Cocotte*, in which Courbet's influence is less evident than in later works, such as *Company at Table*, for example, a work that is very similar to the French artist's *After the Meal* (1849).

The Importance of a Chromatic Palette

In the composition of his paintings, Leibl was a believer

in color, both for its own sake and to a large extent for the depiction of light and shade. He was extraordinarily skilled at drawing, which allowed him to endow his paintings with the firm lineal structure that can be seen in the work of Ingres.

For many years, from the middle of 1870 to the beginning of 1880, Leibl tried to achieve a complete balance between color and line. In his most famous works of this period, such as *Three Women in Church* (1878–1882), he took Naturalism to its extremes, in a composition of axes and intersecting curves.

In some of the paintings he produced around the same period, for example in the two versions of *In the Kitchen* (1898), light becomes a factor of great importance. Many years before, in the portrait *The Painter Sattler with a Hunting Dog*, Leibl had already stressed the importance of light in his art and painted the subject as if it were an impression of light, akin to the technique later developed by the Impressionists.

Leibl's Followers

When Leibl returned to Munich in 1873, the circle of his artist followers lost cohesion. Only his inseparable friend Johann Sperl (1840–1914) remained faithful to him until his death. These artists tried to innovate on the work of their master, focusing on coherent tones and *chiaroscuro* that included effects of light and atmosphere.

From then on, the painters composing Leibl's school in Munich forged a new direction for German painting. Among these painters, only the Viennese artist Carl Schuch (1846–1903) achieved, in some of his still-life paintings, a perfection similar to Leibl's.

In his early works, Wilhelm Trübner (1851–1917) showed that he neared the essence of

Carl Schuch.
Still Life
(1885).
28.5 × 25.75 in.
Neue
Pinakothek,
Munich.

Wilhelm
Trübner.
In the
Artist's Studio
(1872).
24 × 32.25 in.
Neue
Pinakothek,
Munich.

Leibl and Schuch's work (*In Heildelberg Castle*, 1873), not just in the smoothness and delicacy of the palette but also in his pictorial technique. Nevertheless, it soon became evident that the style of both Schuch and Trübner was more intellectual than that of Leibl and Courbet, although many landscapes by the latter artist maintain a great spontaneity in their brush stroke.

Other German painters, such as Theodor Alt (1846–

1937) and Albert von Keller (1844–1920), can also be considered to have been influenced by Courbet and Leibl, although they used tonality to convey other types of feeling.

THE ROAD TO SPANISH REALISM

Romanticism promoted the representation of people and customs germane to specific places, thus identifiable with concrete locations. Having used common, everyday scenes as themes for paintings, the artists' need to generalize their subject matter resulted in a succession of attempts to broaden the reproduction of similar images. These images always preserved the emphasis on observation, clearly stressing the reproduction of the topic's visual truth.

The *Costumbrista* Tradition and the Capture of Reality

After the mid-1800s, the favorite subject matter for *costumbrista* painting expanded beyond characters and customs with a local flavor. Painters began increasingly to focus on the new types of communities and urban spaces in the modern city whose picturesque attractiveness made them well suitable subjects for painting.

In this evolutionary process, typically Romantic *costumbrista* painting remained rooted in Spanish painting traditions that changed only with difficulty. However, from the middle of the century onward, the internalization of painting encouraged the cross-boundary diffusion of themes and fostered in the local character, which pre-served its *costumbrista* genre, a choice of topics or formal treatment that revealed points of view sympathetic to new currents.

The Figure of Ramón Martí Alsina

Born in Barcelona, Martí Alsina (1826–1894) is considered the major representative of an artistic expression very similar to that of Courbet, and thus, Realist. Trained at the Llotja, he was opposed to the Nazarene concepts then in vogue and tended toward the Romantic style painting of Vernet, whose spirit he celebrates in his unfinished work *The Defenders of Gerona*. From an early age he felt drawn to the representation of landscape and of daily life (*Landscape*, 1860).

After losing his job as a teacher at the Llotja because of his opposition to King Amadeo I — although he was later rehabilitated during the First Republic—he painted continuously to be able to support himself.

He had many different studios in Barcelona with numerous apprentices. His best works show evidence of the vitality of the first generation of European Realists. He painted multiple urban scenes, both in Barcelona (such as *El Bornet de Barcelona*, c. 1870) and in other European cities like Paris—a city from which, on one of his visits, he traveled to Belgium and Holland drawn by the work of Rembrandt. He also produced exquisitely painted scenes from daily life (*La Siesta*, c. 1880).

Ramón Martí Alsina. El Bornet de Barcelona (c. 1870).
Oil on canvas, 45 × 22.75 in. Museum of Modern Art, Barcelona.

José Perez Laguna. Palace Courtyard *(1871).*
Oil on canvas, 8.75 × 10.75 in. Private Collection.

painting, which was popularized in France by artists like Meissonier (1815–1891).

Leading Artists

The founders of this new artistic current, including Josep Serra (1828–1910), traveled to Paris around 1860. Serra was a follower of Meissonier in the French capital, although he immediately became linked with the academic life of Barcelona (*The Bookseller's House,* 1857). These artists also had links with the French artist José Pérez Laguna and Luis Ruipérez (1832–1867), the most important member of the group being Eduardo Zamacois (1841–1871), a painter who is considered the first major Spanish representative of this pictorial genre.

Before the fall of the Second Empire, painters like Raimundo de Madrazo and Ignacio de Léon, among other artists, also traveled to Paris, consolidating, with the support of high society, their fame and style during the final quarter of the century.

Small-Scale Genre Painting

Small-scale genre painting owes its existence to a private clientele that provided the socioeconomic base that favored its extraordinary rise to popularity by demanding small paintings for predominantly decorative purposes. The French term *tableautin* — small painting — best defines this type of painting, since it was in France that the works of many artists who painted these small paintings were first sold.

Beginning in the 1860s, a number of innovations began to be appreciated in anecdotal representations that can be described as Realist. This is the case, for example, with the depiction of irrelevant topics, which are characterized by capturing a single moment in the scene depicted or by relying increasingly on compositional resources borrowed

from the Realist genre. It should be noted that the Spanish painters' presence in, or contact with, Paris awoke in them a renewed interest in genre

Raimundo de Madrazo. Portrait of Aline Masson Wearing a Mantilla. *Oil on canvas, 20.5 × 25.5 in. The Prado, Casón del Buen Retiro, Madrid.*

MARIÀ FORTUNY

No other Spanish Romantic painter achieved the international fame of Marià Fortuny, an indisputable reference point in the history of art with ties to the commercial-artistic circles of Paris. Honored both by national and international critics, an example of his standing as an artist was the sobriquet "Fortunystic" given to his models and resources of his paintings.

Fortuny's Training and Early Career

Marià Fortuny. Naked Man on the Beach at Portici *(1874).*
Oil on board, 7.5 × 5.25 in. The Prado, Cason del Buen Retiro, Madrid.

Considered the most international, sought after, admired, and imitated Spanish painter of the nineteenth century, Marià Fortuny (1838–1874) was born in Reus (Spain). He owed his initial training to the Barcelona academy of The Llotja, which he entered with the help of a scholarship in 1852, and to the tutelage he received from his grandfather, his father having died when he was still young.

The Nazarene ethos that flourished at the Llotja, due principally to his teacher Claudio Lorenzale, influenced his youthful works. In 1857, with the work *The Count of Berenguer III Nailing the Ensign of Saint Eulalia into Foix Castle*, he won one of the scholarships offered by the city authorities of Barcelona to study in Rome. Beginning his adventure in the Italian capital the following year, he attended the Academia Chigi and the premises of the Café Greco, along with the colony of Spanish residents there. In 1860, while he was still in Rome, the Barcelona city authorities proposed him for the painting of the heroic gestures of the Catalan volunteers in the war in North Africa. As a result of this commission, he moved to Tetuán, where he painted the work *Battle of Wad-ras.* In 1861 he produced the *Odalisque,* completed in Rome where he moved to paint the large-scale commission *The Battle of Tetuán* (1863).

Marià Fortuny.
Moroccans.
Oil on canvas,
7.5 × 5.25 in.
The Prado,
Madrid.

Marià Fortuny. The Curate's Office (1870).
Oil on canvas, 36.25 × 21.75 in. Museum of Modern Art, Barcelona.

Travels to Paris

Between the years 1865 and 1866 he moved to Paris and began a new stage in his artistic career, thanks to the marketing of his work by the art seller Adolphe Goupil and to being well acquainted with the work of Meissonier through Eduardo Zamacois.

Following his marriage in 1867, he set himself up in Madrid, although he returned to Rome the following year, producing a large number of works during this period, such as *Fantasy on Faust* (1866), *Arabic Fantasy* (1867), and most important of all, *The Curate's Office*, begun in 1867 and completed in 1870, which was described by Théophile Gautier as "a Goya retouched by Meissonier."

Fortuny's Final Years in Rome

Following other journeys and periods of residence, he moved to Italy for good, where the final stages of his life were a period of great activity during which he painted with complete liberty. His style, aided by the interplay of light, achieved a great degree of realism.

During the summer of 1874 he spent time in Portici (Naples), a place where he painted *Naked Man on the Beach at Portici*, which captured, in the open air, the brilliant luminosity of the Mediterranean. Also from this period dates the extremely colorist work *Fortuny's Children in the Japanese Room of his House*. This period was brought to a close by the artist's sudden death in Rome, an event that shocked the artistic communities there and those Paris and Spain.

THE ARTIST'S LIFE

1838 Born in Reus (Spain).
1852–1856 Studies at the School of the Llotja in Barcelona.
1857 Wins a scholarship to study in Rome with the work *The Count of Berenguer III Nailing the Ensign of Saint Eulalia into Foix Castle.*
1858 Moves to Rome, where he has a studio for many years.

1862 Travels to Morocco for the second time, where the end of the conflict allows him to study the atmosphere and climate of the Arab world with calm.
1867 Marries Cecilia, the daughter of Federico Madrazo. Moves to Madrid, where he copies works from The Prado and comes into contact with Madrid artistic circles.
1869–1870 Returns to Paris again, where he works in the studio of Gerôme.
1872 Travels to Morocco again, but quickly returns to Granada and later to Rome, Paris, and London.
1874 Dies in Rome.

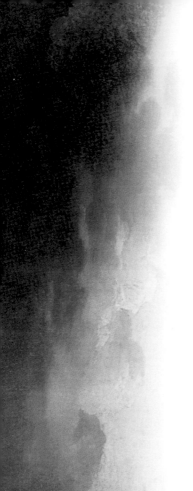

Original title of the book in Spanish: *El Romanticismo*
© Copyright Parramón Ediciones, S.A. 1999—World Rights.
Published by Parramón Ediciones, S.A., Barcelona, Spain.
Author: Parramón's Editorial Team
Illustrators: Parramón's Editorial Team

Copyright of the English edition © 2000 by
Barron's Educational Series, Inc.

All inquiries should be addressed to:
Barron's Educational Series, Inc.
250 Wireless Boulevard
Hauppauge, New York 11788
http://www.barronseduc.com

International Standard Book No. 0-7641-5291-2

Library of Congress Catalog Card No. 00-103322

Printed in Spain
9 8 7 6 5 4 3 2 1

Front cover:
Théodore Géricault. *Hussar Officer Ordering a Charge* (detail).
Dante Gabriel Rossetti. *Prosperine* (detail).
Caspar David Friedrich. *Stages of Life* (detail).

Back cover:
Friedrich Overbeck. *Vittoria Caldoni da Albano* (detail).
Edward Coley Burne-Jones. *The Beguiling of Merlin* (detail).

Note: The titles that appear at the top of the
odd-numbered pages correspond to:

The previous chapter
The current chapter
The following chapter